BOOK ONE

The Grammar Lab

Kenna Bourke

Illustrated by Korky Paul and David Mostyn

OXFORD

UNIVERSITY PRESS

OXFORD
UNIVERSITY PRESS

Great Clarendon Street, Oxford OX2 6DP

Oxford University Press is a department of the University of Oxford.
It furthers the University's objective of excellence in research, scholarship,
and education by publishing worldwide in

Oxford New York

Auckland Cape Town Dar es Salaam Hong Kong Karachi
Kuala Lumpur Madrid Melbourne Mexico City Nairobi
New Delhi Shanghai Taipei Toronto

With offices in

Argentina Austria Brazil Chile Czech Republic France Greece
Guatemala Hungary Italy Japan Poland Portugal Singapore
South Korea Switzerland Thailand Turkey Ukraine Vietnam

OXFORD and OXFORD ENGLISH are registered trade marks of
Oxford University Press in the UK and in certain other countries

ISBN-13: 978 0 19 433015 2

Typeset in New Baskerville and Gill Sans

Printed in China

ACKNOWLEDGEMENTS
Designed by Richard Morris, Stonesfield Design, Oxfordshire

www.korkypaul.com

Splodge
Splodge lives in Wibble with Ruff and Tumble.
He's got a rabbit called Sticky.
He eats mud pies and drinks Fizzy Ink.
He reads *Mo and Snapper* comics.

Ruff
Ruff is an inventor. He's got a lab.
He makes magic potions and
machines, like his world-famous
Boomerang Biscuit machine.

Tumble
Tumble is kind.
He helps Splodge.
He reads books and newspapers.
He also sleeps a lot.

Mabel
Mabel lives next door to Splodge with
her friend Mildred. She loves tortoises.
She's got a big red nose
and straight hair.

Mildred
Mildred's nose is pointed,
like a carrot. Her hair is curly.
She likes parrots.

Contents

Articles

1 Tick (✔) the correct boxes.

* How many Articles are there in the picture?
  Three ☐   Two ☐   One ☐

* What are the names of the Articles?
  Splodge ☐   A ☐   Sticky ☐   An ☐

 GRAMMAR

A

a and **an** can tell you what a person, animal or thing is.

> *I'm **a** pupil.*
> *Ruff is **an** inventor.*
> *Sticky is **a** rabbit.*
> *That's **an** octopus.*
> *A dictionary is **a** book.*

2 Read and guess what the person is.
Tick the correct box.

Mrs Fixit likes animals. When they're ill, she gives them food, drink and medicine. Today she's giving a dog some medicine.

She's …
a singer. ☐   a teacher. ☐
a vet (an animal doctor). ☐

REMEMBER!

These are vowels: **a, e, i, o, u**

These are consonants:

b, c, d, f, g, h, j, k, l, m, n, p, q, r, s, t, v, w, x, y, z

See Chapter 38.

3 Write two words beginning with a vowel, and two words beginning with a consonant.

▶ elephant................ green.........................

....

....

B

Put **a** before a consonant when you want to talk about *one* thing.

> *a dog, a rabbit, a table, a pen*
> *Splodge has got a rabbit.*
> *This is a book.*
> *It's a blue pen.*

4 Fill in the gaps.

Splodge's rabbit has got ▶ a...... nice face and long ears. It's got (1) .... black tail. It lives in (2) .... big box in Splodge's bedroom. Every day Splodge gives his rabbit (3) .... carrot and (4) .... biscuit.

C

Put **an** before a vowel when you want to talk about *one* thing.

> *an umbrella, an elephant, an egg, an apple*
> *That's an umbrella.*
> *I'm cooking an egg.*
> *Splodge wants an apple.*

5 Put in the correct article.

▶ Splodge makes mud pies with an.... egg.

1 Splodge has got .... elephant. It's a toy elephant.

2 Ruff is hungry. He's eating .... orange.

3 Now he's eating .... apple.

4 Mabel often carries .... umbrella, even in summer.

D

Be careful! Learn these.

a useful book	NOT	~~an useful book~~
a uniform	NOT	~~an uniform~~
an hour	NOT	~~a hour~~

6 Fill in the gaps. Use **a** or **an**.

Splodge goes to school. He doesn't wear (1) .... uniform at school. He wears T-shirts. He likes school, but he doesn't like homework. Every day Splodge does homework for (2) .... hour. He likes English. He says a grammar book is (3) .... useful book.

PRACTICE

7

a **A** or **an**? Make two lists.

article ✔   dog ✔   tree
ear   egg   girl
lesson   boy   uncle
face   house   artist
bicycle   head   arm
hour   toy   orange
owl   eye   cat   apple

a	**an**
► *a dog*	*an article* ...
....	....
....	....
....	....
....	....
....	....
....	....
....	....
....	....
....	....

b Work with a partner. Take turns to test each other. Use the words in **7a**.

► Partner A   *Dog.*
   Partner B   *A dog.*

   Partner B   *Article.*
   Partner A   *An article.*

8 Fill in the gaps. Use **a** or **an**.

Splodge   Can Sticky have ► *a* ...... carrot?

Ruff   Yes, there are some in the kitchen.

Splodge   Can I give him (1) .... apple and (2) .... biscuit?

Ruff   Yes. Is he very hungry?

Splodge   He's always hungry. Can he have (3) .... banana milkshake, too?

Ruff   No. Rabbits don't like milkshakes.

Splodge   Oh, that's strange. Can he have (4) .... egg, then?

Ruff   No. Rabbits don't eat eggs.

Splodge   He wants (5) .... orange. Have we got oranges?

Ruff   No, Splodge. Don't be silly. Give Sticky (6) .... carrot and go and read (7) .... book.

Splodge   I don't want to. Can I go outside?

Ruff   Yes, but it's raining. Take (8) .... umbrella.

Splodge   Sticky is coming with me. We want to play (9) .... game.

Ruff   All right, but come back in (10) .... hour and don't give Sticky any more food!

9 Ask your teacher if you can play this game. Imagine you are in Splodge's house. What can you see? You can say anything you like. Play the game like this:

► Pupil A   *In Splodge's house I see a chair.*
   Pupil B   *In Splodge's house I see a chair and an elephant.*
   Pupil C   *In Splodge's house I see a chair, an elephant and an apple.*
   Pupil D   *In Splodge's house I see a chair, an elephant, an apple and a rabbit.*

Demonstratives

I made **this** beautiful pot.

Look here! I made **these** lovely plates.

What are **those** things?

Pot

Plates

Painting

Statues

That painting is Ruff's. It's ugly. He can't paint.

1   Tick (✔) the correct box.

Where's Splodge's pot?
Near him ☐   Not near him ☐

G GRAMMAR

A

this and **these** are to talk about people or things that are near you.

One	Two or more
This is my beautiful pot.	*These* are my pots.
This pot is beautiful.	*These* pots are beautiful.

2   Fill in the gaps. Use **this** and **these**.

▶ ..This...... is Splodge's painting of a rabbit.

(1) .... are his pink and blue pots.

Splodge likes them very much. (2) ....

is his best painting and (3) .... are

his favourite statues. Splodge doesn't like

(4) .... square plate: it's Ruff's!

B

that and **those** are to talk about people or things that are far from you.

One	Two or more
That's Ruff's statue.	*Those are Ruff's statues.*
That statue is Ruff's.	*Those statues are Ruff's.*

3 Look at the conversation. Put in **that** and **those**.

Splodge   Who are ▶ *those* .... ladies?

Ruff   They're artists. They live in Wibble. Be polite to them!

Splodge   What's (1) .... ? It looks horrible!

Ruff   Shhh! It's Tumble's new painting.

Splodge   Look, (2) .... people are looking at my beautiful statue!

Ruff   Yes, but look at (3) .... woman over there.

Splodge   Which woman? Oh, the woman looking at (4) .... strange pots?

Ruff   They're not pots! They're my best statues!

 PRACTICE

4

a Look at the words below.
Write sentences with **be** and **this** or **these**.

Splodge's paintings ✔	Ruff's plates
my best drawing ✔	Splodge's statue
ugly statues	Tumble's pot
your paintbrush	my neighbours
Ruff's friend	a beautiful drawing
new pictures	horrible colours

this

▶ *This is my best drawing.* ....

....

....

....

....

these

These are Splodge's paintings. ....

....

....

....

....

b Work with a partner. Take turns to say two sentences with **this** and two sentences with **these**. You can talk about anything you like.

▶ Partner A   *This is my pencil case.*
Partner B   *This is Splodge's desk.*

Partner A   *These are my ears.*
Partner B   *These are my hands.*

5 Fill in the gaps. Use **that** or **those**.

Ruff   Where are you going, Splodge?

Splodge   Umm. I'm going outside to paint a picture. Give me ▶ *those* comics and some chocolate, please. Oh, no! Look at (1) .... clouds. I can't paint in the rain. Pass me (2) .... umbrella please, Ruff.

Ruff   Which umbrella?

Splodge   (3) .... yellow one over there by the door.

Ruff   Here you are. But Splodge, what are you doing with (4) .... cheese and (5) .... enormous sandwiches?

Splodge   What sandwiches?

Ruff   (6) .... sandwiches! The enormous sandwiches under your hat.

Splodge   Oh, yes. I remember. An artist needs lots of food. I'm a famous painter! Now, pass me (7) .... apples and (8) .... bag of sweets.

Ruff   Splodge, what's in (9) .... box by the door?

Splodge   Oh, yes, (10) .... is my rabbit. He wants to paint. I'm teaching him. We need some extra sweets and sandwiches for him. He's always hungry when he paints.

6 Ask your teacher if you can play a class game. One pupil starts the game. Imagine that the pupil is a visitor from another planet. The pupil walks round the classroom asking questions. The class tells him or her what each thing is. Play the game like this:

▶ Pupil   *What's this?* (Pupil points at a desk.)
Class   *It's a desk.*
Pupil   *What are these?*
(Pupil points at some books.)
Class   *They're books.*
Pupil   *What's that?*
(Pupil points at the window.)
Class   *It's a window.*
Pupil   *What are those?*
(Pupil points at the clouds.)
Class   *They're clouds.*

When the 'visitor' has asked four questions, choose another pupil to play the game.

Possessives

Splodge, you need this.
It's Splodge's rabbit, Mabel's cat and Mildred's parrot.

1 Tick (✔) the correct boxes.

• Is Splodge making mistakes?
   Yes ☐   No ☐

• Which sentence is correct?
   It's Splodge rabbit. ☐
   It's Splodge's rabbit. ☐

GRAMMAR

A

's and **'** are to tell you who owns something.

    This is Splodge's rabbit.
    This is Ruff's machine.
    These are the boys' bicycles.
    These are women's shoes.

2 Read the sentences. Answer the questions.

1 Splodge's rabbit is called Sticky.

   Who owns the rabbit? ....

2 The rabbit's ears are long.

   Who has got long ears? ....

REMEMBER!

You can count most nouns.

One (Singular)	Two or more (Plural)
a banana	*three bananas*
a crocodile	*ten crocodiles*
an orange	*oranges*
a boy	*boys*
a house	*houses*

See Chapter 8.

3 Write three singular nouns and three plural nouns.

Singular	Plural
► *a girl*	*girls*
....	....
....	....
....	....

B

Put **'s** after singular nouns and people's names.

Singular nouns	People's names
The rabbit's ears are long.	*Splodge's rabbit is called Sticky.*
The boy's bicycle is new.	*Tumble's clothes are funny.*

4 Fill in the gaps.

► It's *Mabel's* (Mabel) cat.

This is my *brother's* (brother) bedroom.

1 This is .... (Splodge) house.

2 It's my .... (friend) bicycle.

3 Where's .... (Ruff) book?

4 The .... (teacher) car is red.

C

Put **'** after plural nouns.

The boys' bicycles are red.
These are our neighbours' friends.
This is the monkeys' cage.

5 Make sentences. Use the words below.

► monkeys / cage
1 teachers / room   3 pupils / books
2 neighbours / cat 4 boys / games

► This cage is the *monkeys' cage.* ....

1 This room is the ....

2 That cat is our........................

3 These books are the ....

4 These games are the........................

D

Be careful! Put **'s** after these plural nouns:

men → *men's*	women → *women's*
children → *children's*	people → *people's*

These are men's shirts.
Those are the children's toys.

6 Rewrite these sentences.

► These are shirts for men.

These are *men's shirts.* ....

1 These are necklaces for women.

These are ....

2 Those are trousers for men.

Those are ....

3 Are these toys for children?

Are these ....

 PRACTICE

7 Match the sentences.

▶ Splodge owns the rabbit.   Their neighbours' car is green.
1 Ruff likes his new machine.   It's the penguins' pool.
2 Their neighbours have got a green car.   Is your parents' garden big?
3 The penguins live in a big pool.   It's Mabel's tortoise.
4 Have your parents got a big garden?   It's Splodge's.
5 Mabel owns a tortoise.   It's Ruff's new machine.

6 Those boys own three skateboards.   It's Mildred's new dress.
7 The elephant has got a long nose.   Splodge's sandwich is big.
8 Mildred has got a new dress.   The elephant's nose is long.
9 Splodge is eating a big sandwich.   The girl's hair is brown.
10 This girl has got brown hair.   They're the boys' skateboards.

8

a Add **'s** or **'**.

▶ cat's   the teachers
▶ the cats'   my mother
   the neighbours   the doctor
   men   the penguins
   a postman   her parents
   the girls   Splodge
   the head teacher   my brother
   my sisters   the dog
   my dentist   the children
   my grandmother   my friends
   the rabbit   his uncle
   our neighbour   a nurse
   your grandparents   women

b Now finish these sentences.

▶ The .....cat's..... (cat) fur is brown.
1 .... (Splodge) favourite food is mud pies.
2 Splodge is going to a .... (children) party.
3 His .... (rabbit) ears are long.
4 .... (Mildred) parrot is funny.
5 Her .... (mother) name is Mary.
6 Splodge's .... (neighbours) house is big.
7 The .... (teachers) room is very noisy.
8 Where's the .... (penguins) cage?
9 Is Splodge wearing .... (women) shoes?
10 Is that the .... (doctor) car?

9

a Fill in the gaps.

Tumble What are these things, Splodge?

Splodge This is ► .Sticky's......... (Sticky) carrot,

and that's (1) .... (Mildred) newspaper.

Tumble Why have you got our (2) .... (neighbours) newspaper?

Splodge Because I need it!

Tumble And what are these?

Splodge Oh, they're (3) .... (children) comics. And that's

(4) .... (Ruff) secret book. I'm making a magic potion.

Tumble What are these?

Splodge They're (5) .... (women) shoes! Can't you see? They're

(6) .... (Mabel) shoes. That's the (7) .... (parrot) toy,

these are my (8) .... (friends) pencils, and that's my

(9) .... (aunt) hat. Now stop asking questions, Tumble.

Tumble But you haven't got an aunt! Is that (10) .... (Ruff) shirt?

Splodge No, it's yours!

b Read **9a** again. Answer the questions.

►	Whose carrot is it?	It's .Sticky's carrot...........
1	Whose secret book is it?	It's ....
2	Whose toy is it?	It's the ....
3	Whose pencils are they?	They're Splodge's ....
4	Whose hat is it?	It's Splodge's ....
5	Whose shirt is it?	It's ....

10 Ask your teacher if you can play this game. Give your teacher
something you own. For example, a pencil, a jumper, a watch.
Don't let the class see what you're giving.
Now take turns to guess who owns each thing.

► Pupil A *Is it Richard's pencil case?*
Teacher *No, it isn't.*

Pupil B *Is it Maria's pencil case?*
Teacher *Yes, it is.*

Possessive adjectives

1 Tick (✔) the correct box.

Who owns the watch?   Mo ☐   Spike (the other boy) ☐

GRAMMAR

REMEMBER!

These are subject pronouns.

I	*I'm happy.*
you	*He's a crocodile.*
he	*We're friends.*
she	
it	
we	
you	
they	

See Chapter 9.

2 Circle the subject pronouns.

(I)'m Snapper. I'm a crocodile. This is Mo. He's my friend. He's got a nice family. They live in a small house in England. Mo has got a sister. She's very young. She's called Milly.

A

Possessive adjectives tell you who owns something.

I've got a sister.	→	*This is **my** sister.*
Spike has got a watch.	→	*It's **his** watch.*
Milly has got a name.	→	***Her** name is Milly.*
We've got toys.	→	*These are **our** toys.*

3 Fill in the gaps.

▶ I've got a cat.

It's my............ cat.

1 I've got a skateboard.

It's .... skateboard.

2 You've got a bicycle.

It's .... bicycle.

3 Milly has got a comic.

It's .... comic.

4 We've got some sweets.

They're .... sweets.

B

These are possessive adjectives.

my	*My* name is Snapper.
your	He's *your* friend.
his	This is *her* bicycle.
her	
its	
our	
your	
their	

4   Complete the table.

Subject pronoun	Possessive adjective
I	my
you	
	his
she	
it	
	our
you	
they	

C

whose is to ask who owns something.

Whose is this watch?	It's his watch.
Whose are these keys?	They're her keys.
Whose T-shirt is this?	It's your T-shirt.
Whose comics are these?	They're my comics.

See Chapter 36.

5   Write four questions. Use **whose** and the words below.

pen ✔ cat shoe bedroom book

▶ Whose is this pen?   OR Whose pen is this?

....

....

....

....

PRACTICE

6

a   Answer the questions.

▶   What's your name?
1   What's your favourite colour?
2   What's your teacher's name?
3   Who's your friend's favourite singer?
4   What's your best friend's name?
5   What's your favourite subject at school?
6   When's your birthday?
7   What's your favourite fruit?
8   What's the name of your school?
9   What's your favourite animal?
10 What's your favourite food?

▶   My name is Maria. ....

1   ....

2   ....

3   ....

4   ....

5   ....

6   ....

7   ....

8   ....

9   ....

10 ....

b   Work with a partner. Take turns to ask and answer the questions.

▶ Partner A	*What's your name?*
Partner B	*My name is …*
Partner B	*What's your favourite colour?*
Partner A	*My favourite colour is …*

7

a Think about your teacher. What are his or her favourite things? Try to guess. Write your answers below.

▶ Number: *Her favourite number is ten.*

Colour: ....

Country: ....

Music: ....

Food: ....

Drink: ....

Television programme: ....

....

Fruit: ....

Animal: ....

Month: ....

Day of the week: ....

....

b Now take turns round the class to ask your teacher if you are right.

▶ Pupil A   *Is your favourite number ten?*
Teacher   *No, it isn't.*
Pupil B   *Is your favourite number four?*
Teacher   *No, it isn't.*
Pupil C   *Is your favourite number seven?*
Teacher   *Yes, it is!*

8 Work with a partner. Draw a monster or a strange animal in the space below. Take turns to draw parts of your monster. When you've finished, describe your picture to the class. Use **our**.

▶ *Our monster has got three legs.*
Our monster has got green eyes.
Our monster has got red hair.

9

a Work in small groups. Invent some characters for a comic. You need a girl, a boy and an animal. First draw your characters on a sheet of paper. Now write a description of each character, like this:

► Name: *Her name is Flops.* ....

Colour of hair: *Her hair is brown.* ....

Girl

Name: ....

Colour of hair: ....

Colour of eyes: ....

Favourite sport: ....

....

Favourite food: ....

....

Favourite music: ....

....

Boy

Name: ....

Colour of hair: ....

Colour of eyes: ....

Favourite sport: ....

....

Favourite food: ....

....

Favourite music: ....

....

Animal

Name: ....

Favourite food: ....

....

Colour: ....

Favourite place: ....

....

b Swap books with another group. Take turns to tell the class about the characters.

► Pupil A   *Their boy's name is Charlie.*
            His hair is red.
            His eyes are blue.

10 Ask your teacher if you can play a guessing game. Think of a person the whole class knows. It can be a famous person or someone in the class. This is how you play the game:

► Pupil A   *His hair is brown.*
Class   *Is it the teacher?*
Pupil A   *No, his shirt is blue.*
Class   *Is it Peter?*
Pupil A   *No, his trousers are blue.*
Class   *Is it George?*
Pupil A   *Yes, it is.*

Possessive pronouns

1   Tick (✔) the correct box.

Who has got the coin now?
Milly ☐   Snapper ☐   Mo ☐

REMEMBER!

These are possessive adjectives.

my	*It's **my** coin.*
your	*It's **her** bicycle.*
his	*It's **our** house.*
her	
its	
our	
your	
their	

See Chapter 4.

2   Write the correct possessive adjective in the gaps.

▶   It's Mo's bicycle. It's *his*......... bicycle.

1   This is Milly's skateboard. It's .... skateboard.

2   Here's Mo and Snapper's house. It's .... house.

3   That's Snapper's coin. It's .... coin.

4   I own this dog. It's .... dog.

REMEMBER!

Pronouns replace nouns.

Noun	Pronoun	
Milly is nice.	*She's nice.*	(***She*** = subject pronoun)
I like **Milly**.	*I like **her**.*	(***her*** = object pronoun)

See Chapter 9.

3   Circle the pronouns.

[We] like Snapper. He's funny. He's Mo's best friend. They like playing football. Mo has got a little sister. She's called Milly. Snapper likes her. They often play games together.

A

Possessive pronouns tell you who owns something.
They replace possessive adjectives and nouns.

They're **my toys**. → *They're **mine**.*
It's **his book**. → *It's **his**.*
It's **our house**. → *It's **ours**.*

4 Which is the correct pronoun?
Tick the boxes.

► It's Mo's book.

It's mine. ☐   It's his. ☑

1 This is Milly's dress.

It's his. ☐   It's hers. ☐

2 That's our house.

It's ours. ☐   It's his. ☐

3 It's his toy.

It's hers. ☐   It's his. ☐

4 This is Milly's radio.

It's hers. ☐   It's mine. ☐

B

These are possessive pronouns.

mine	*This bicycle is **mine**.*
yours	*This book is **his**.*
his	*These comics are **ours**.*
hers	
ours	
yours	
theirs	

5 Fill in the gaps.

Possessive adjectives + noun	Possessive pronouns
my book	► mine
your sister	....
his comic	....
her skateboard	....
our house	....
your cat	....
their radio	....

C

whose is to ask who owns something.

***Whose** is this book?*	It's Mo's.
***Whose** are these shoes?*	They're mine.
***Whose** car is that?*	It's his.
***Whose** toys are these?*	They're ours.

See Chapter 36.

6 Write four questions with **whose**.
Use the words below.

pencil ✔   football   jacket
dictionary   bicycle

► Whose is this pencil? OR Whose pencil is this?

....

....

....

....

PRACTICE

THESE ARE SNAPPER'S CHOCOLATES.

7 Match the sentences.

► This is our house.   It's mine.

1 These are Snapper's chocolates.   They're theirs.

2 Mo's friends have got skateboards.   It's his.

3 This is Mo's bicycle.   They're his.

4 These are our comics.   It's ours.

5 It's my dog.   They're ours.

---

6 Those are Milly's puzzle books.   It's mine.

7 It's your birthday present.   It's hers.

8 They're our games.   They're hers.

9 That's my football.   It's yours.

10 This is her picture.   They're ours.

8 Read the sentences. Fill in the gaps with the correct possessive pronoun.

► Mo has got a blue T-shirt.   It's his.

1 Milly has got three hats.   They're ....

2 These are Snapper's toys.   They're ....

3 This is Mo's mother's car.   It's ....

4 You've got a green car.   It's ....

5 That's Snapper and Mo's room.   It's ....

6 These are our games.   They're ....

7 I've got a black and white cat.   It's ....

8 They've got a swing.   It's ....

9 We've got bicycles.   They're ....

10 Mo's sister has got a new comic.   It's ....

9

a Look at the picture. Answer the questions. Use possessive pronouns.

▶ Are the comics Milly's?

No, they aren't hers. They're Spike's.

Is the football Mo and Snapper's?

Yes, it's theirs.

1 Is the bicycle Milly's?

....

2 Is the doll Mo and Snapper's?

....

3 Is the telephone Milly's?

....

4 Is the chocolate Spike's?

....

5 Is the radio Milly's?

....

6 Are the clothes Spike's?

....

7 Is the skateboard Milly's?

....

8 Is the apple Milly's?

....

9 Is the book Spike's?

....

10 Is the dog Mo and Snapper's?

....

b Work with a partner. Look at the picture again for one minute. Partner B, shut your book. Partner A, ask questions about whose the things are.

▶ Partner A *Whose is the skateboard?*
  Partner B *It's Milly's.*

Now, Partner A, shut your book. Partner B, ask questions.

10 Ask your teacher if you can play a class game. Give your teacher one thing that you own, for example a watch, a pencil, a jacket. Now answer your teacher's questions.

▶ Teacher *Is this Antony's jacket?*
  Pupil A *No, it's mine.*

  Teacher *Whose is this watch?*
  Pupil B *It's his.* (Point at the person you think owns the watch.)

Quantifiers 1

Splodge! What are you doing?

Seven, eight, nine ... I'm counting sugar.

You can't count sugar. It's impossible.

1 Tick (✔) the correct boxes.

- You can't count sugar.
  Can you count salt?   Yes ☐   No ☐

- You can count apples.
  Can you count bananas?   Yes ☐   No ☐

 GRAMMAR

REMEMBER!

Nouns you can count		Nouns you can't count
One	Two or more	
a cat	*three cats*	*bread*
an egg	*five eggs*	*cheese*

See Chapter 8.

2 Write four more nouns.
Put them in the correct column.

Nouns you can count	Nouns you can't count
three eggs	salt
a house	music
....	....
....	....

A

If there's only one thing, use **a** or **an**.

*Splodge is making **a** cake.*
*Tumble has got **a** newspaper.*
*I'm eating **an** apple.*
*Is there **an** egg in the fridge?*

See Chapter 1.

3 This is Splodge's recipe for fruit salad.
Fill in the gaps. Use **a** or **an**.

▶ A........ pear and (1) .... orange.

(2) .... apple, (3) .... banana and

(4) .... peach.

B

If there's more than one thing and it's easy to
count, use a number.

*Splodge has got **two** apples.*
*There are **five** biscuits on the plate.*

See Chapter 10.

4 Answer the questions.

▶ How many legs have you got?

I've got two legs.

1 Have you got three ears?

No, I've got ....

2 How many pupils are there in your class?

There are ....

in my class.

3 How many fingers have you got?

I've got ....

4 How many legs has a dog got?

A dog has got ....

C

If there's more than one thing but you don't
know exactly how many or it isn't important how
many, use **some**.

*I've got **some** eggs.*
*There are **some** oranges in the kitchen.*
*Splodge is eating **some** mud pies.*

5 Splodge is cooking. Look at the words below.
What does he need? Write sentences.
Use **some**.

eggs ✔   bananas   carrots   onions
tomatoes

▶ He needs some eggs.

....

....

....

....

D

You can also use **some** with nouns you
can't count.

*There's **some** apple juice in the fridge.*
*There's **some** sugar in the cupboard.*

6 Put the words in the correct order.

▶ chocolate   There's   some   in

cupboard.   the

There's some chocolate in the cupboard.

1 milk   in   the   There's   some   fridge.

....

2 There's   bread.   some

....

3 I've   some   got   cheese.

....

4 table.   butter   on   There's   some   the

....

7

a **A**, **an** or **some**? Cross out the wrong words.

Splodge   I'm hungry. How do you make a sandwich?

Tumble   To make a cheese and tomato sandwich

you need ► a̶/some bread, (1) some/a tomato,

(2) some/a butter and (3) some/a cheese.

Splodge   I don't like tomatoes! Tumble, I'm thirsty.

Can I have (4) an/some apple juice?

Tumble   No. You can have (5) some/a milk and

(6) a/some biscuit. Then you can help me. I'm making

(7) some/a tea and (8) a/some cakes for Ruff.

Splodge   How do you make cakes?

Tumble   You need (9) a/some flour, (10) a/some sugar,

(11) some/a butter and (12) an/some egg.

Splodge   You make the cakes. I want some chocolate!

b Work with a partner. Take turns to ask and answer
the questions.

► What do you need to make a sandwich? (Say two things.)
1 What does Splodge want to drink?
2 Splodge can't have apple juice. What can he have?
3 What's Tumble making? (Say two things.)
4 What do you need to make cakes? (Say three things.)

► Partner A   *What do you need to make a sandwich?*
  Partner B   *You need some bread and some butter.*

  Partner B   *What does Splodge want to drink?*
  Partner A   *He wants …*

8

a What's in Tumble's cupboard?
Look at the things in the picture.
Write ten sentences. Use **some**.

► *There are some potatoes.*
  There's some lemonade.

....

....

....

....

....

....

....

....

b Work with a partner. Look at the picture in **8a** for one minute. Partner A, shut your book. Say all the things you can remember.
Now Partner B, shut your book. Say all the things you can remember.

▶ Partner A   *There are some eggs and some carrots. There's some sugar, some milk and some cheese.*

    Partner B   *There's some bread and some milk. There are some carrots …*

9

a Can you cook? Write answers to the questions.

▶ What do you need to make a sandwich?
  You need some bread and some butter.

1 What do you need to make a mushroom omelette?

  ....
  ....

2 What do you need to make a strawberry milkshake?

  ....
  ....

3 What do you need to make a cheese and tomato pizza?

  ....
  ....

4 What do you need to make a banana and chocolate sandwich?

  ....
  ....

5 What do you need to make chicken and vegetable soup?

  ....
  ....

b Think of three things that you like to eat. Work with a partner. Ask your partner to guess what you need to make your things.

▶ Partner A   *Pea soup.*
    Partner B   *You need some peas and some water.*

    Partner B   *Chocolate biscuits.*
    Partner A   *You need some sugar, some flour and some chocolate.*

10 Work with a partner. Choose a recipe from Splodge's book. Take turns to say what you need for each recipe.

VERY BORING SANDWICH
bread, butter, cheese

CARROT AND BANANA SOUP
water, carrots, one banana

FIZZY INK
water, black ink, 3 apples

GREEN PEA MILKSHAKE
peas, milk, sugar, one egg

FANTASTIC ORANGE BUBBLEGUM
chocolate, oranges, water, glue

ONION LOLLIPOPS
four onions, salt, CHEESE, SUGAR

CHOCOLATE TOOTHPASTE
toothpaste, chocolate, sugar

STRAWBERRY SNOW
eggs, milk, NINE BIG strawberries

MEAT AND HONEY BURGERS
honey, onions, meat, rice

▶ Partner A   *A Very Boring Sandwich.*
    Partner B   *You need some bread, some butter and some cheese.*

    Partner B   *Carrot and Banana Soup.*
    Partner A   *You need some water, some carrots and a banana.*

Quantifiers 2

Sorry, Splodge. You can't have a banana sandwich. There isn't **any** bread and there aren't **any** bananas.

No bread, no bananas! Life is terrible.

1 Tick (✔) the correct box.

Splodge can't have a sandwich because …
Ruff is angry. ☐   there's no bread. ☐

GRAMMAR

REMEMBER!

Use **a** and **some** with nouns you can count.
Use **some** with nouns you can't count.

Nouns you can count	Nouns you can't count
a banana	*some bread*
some bananas	*some cheese*

See Chapter 8.

2 Fill in the gaps. Use **a** or **some**.

Splodge   Are there any apples?

Ruff   Yes, there are (1) ………… apples

in the bowl.

Splodge   Is there any cheese?

Ruff   Yes, there's (2) ………… cheese here.

A

Use **any** to ask questions with nouns.

*Are there **any** apples?*
*Have we got **any** oranges?*
*Is there **any** milk?*
*Have we got **any** bread?*

3 Write four questions.
Use **any** and the words below.

apples ✔   bread ✔   cheese   sweets
sugar   oranges

▸ Are there any apples?

Is there any bread?

....

....

....

....

B

Do you want to know exactly what number there are?
Use **how many** to ask questions with nouns you can count.

> *How many bananas are there?*
> *How many toys has Splodge got?*
> *How many sandwiches can Splodge eat?*

See Chapter 35.

4 Write questions. Use **how many** and the words below.

You want to know the number of …

days there are in a week ✔
apples there are in the bowl
biscuits Tumble eats every day
friends Splodge has got
minutes there are in an hour

▶ How many days .... are there in a week?

1 .... are there in the bowl?

2 .... does Tumble eat every day?

3 .... has Splodge got?

4 .... are there in an hour?

C

Use **how much** to ask questions with nouns you can't count.

> *How much milk is there?*
> *How much water can you drink?*
> *How much cheese does Ruff eat every day?*

See Chapter 35.

5 Match the questions to the answers.

▶ How much water can Ruff drink in a minute?   You need two cups of black ink.

1 How much ink do you need to make Fizzy Ink?   He can drink a litre.

2 How much bread does Tumble eat every day?   He drinks ten litres a week.

3 How much cheese does Splodge put in a sandwich?   He puts half a kilo in his sandwich.

4 How much milk does Splodge drink every week?   He eats two loaves of bread.

D

Use **any** in negative sentences.

Negative –	Positive +
*No, there aren't **any** bananas.*	Yes, there are some bananas.
*No, there aren't **any** sandwiches.*	Yes, there are some sandwiches.
*No, we haven't got **any** milk.*	Yes, there's some milk.
*No, we haven't got **any** bread.*	Yes, there's some bread.

6 Write four negative sentences. Use **any**.

► *There isn't any milk.* .... (milk)

 There aren't any sweets. .... (sweets)

1 .... (bread)

2 .... (apples)

3 .... (cheese)

4 .... (oranges)

 PRACTICE

7

a Splodge wants to go shopping. He's asking Ruff questions. Write Ruff's answers. Use **any**.

Splodge   Are there any bananas? Have we got any bread?

Ruff   No, ► *there aren't any bananas.* ....

   No, we haven't got any bread. ....

Splodge   Have we got any sweets?

Ruff   No, (1) ....

Splodge   Are there any biscuits?

Ruff   No, (2) ....

Splodge   Is there any rice?

Ruff   No, (3) ....

Splodge   Are there any pineapples?

Ruff   No, (4) ....

Splodge   Have we got any honey?

Ruff   No, (5) ....

Splodge   Can you give me some money? I need to buy lots of

   things! There isn't any food in the house.

b Work with a partner. Partner A, you're Ruff. Partner B, you're Splodge. Ask and answer the questions in **7a**.

► Partner A   *Are there any bananas?*

 Partner B   *No, there aren't any bananas.*

8

a How much or **how many**? Fill in the gaps.

▶ ~~How much~~...... money have you got?

  ~~How many~~...... apples do we need?

1 .... sandwiches do we need?

2 .... oranges do we need?

3 .... cheese does Ruff want?

4 .... sweets can Splodge have?

5 .... milk is there in the fridge?

6 .... salt does Splodge want to buy?

7 .... bananas do you want?

8 .... apple juice can Ruff drink?

9 .... eggs can Splodge eat?

10 .... sugar do you put in a cake?

b Work with a partner. Take turns to test each other. Make questions using the words in the list below and **how much** or **how many**.

meat ✔ cherries ✔ water salt milk
apples sweets cheese biscuits bread
sandwiches tomatoes butter potatoes

▶ Partner A *Meat.*
  Partner B *How much meat is there?*

  Partner B *Cherries.*
  Partner A *How many cherries are there?*

9 Make the positive sentences negative. Use **any**.

▶ Yes, there are some biscuits.
  ~~No, there aren't any biscuits.~~
  Yes, there's some milk.
  ~~No, there isn't any milk.~~

1 Yes, there's some cheese.
  ....

2 Yes, there are some tomatoes.
  ....

3 Yes, there are some oranges.
  ....

4 Yes, there's some orange juice.
  ....

5 Yes, there's some salt.
  ....

6 Yes, there are some sweets.
  ....

7 Yes, there's some coffee.
  ....

8 Yes, there's some sugar.
  ....

9 Yes, there are some bananas.
  ....

10 Yes, there are some sandwiches.
  ....

10 Ask your teacher if you can play a class game. Listen carefully to what your friends say! Play the game like this:

▶ Pupil A *In Splodge's kitchen I see some bread.*
  Pupil B *In Splodge's kitchen I see some bread and an apple.*
  Pupil C *In Splodge's kitchen I see some bread, an apple and five bananas.*
  Pupil D *In Splodge's kitchen I see some bread, an apple, five bananas and some cheese.*

REVISION 1 – articles; demonstratives; possessives

1 Read the sentences and cross out the wrong words in the rules below.

There's an animal. It's a tiger!

Put **an** before a consonant / vowel .

Put **a** before a consonant / vowel .

2 These sentences are wrong. Correct them.

Splodge never wears an uniform.

....

He's going to school in a hour.

....

An atlas is an useful book.

....

3 Read the examples and tick the correct boxes.

This is my hand. These are my fingers.
That's the sun. Those are the stars.

This and **these** are for things …
that are near you.   ☐
that are far from you.   ☐

That and **those** are for things …
that are near you.   ☐
that are far from you.   ☐

4 Fill in the gaps. Use **this** or **these**.

.... are my sweets.

.... is my bedroom.

5 Fill in the gaps. Use **that** or **those**.

.... is the playground.

.... are my friends.

6 Read the sentences and answer the questions.

Sticky is Splodge's rabbit.
The boy's cat is black.
The red pens are the girls' pens.

Who owns the rabbit? ....

Who owns the cat? ....

Who owns the pens? ....

7 Cross out the wrong answers.

Put ' / 's after people's names and

singular nouns.

Put ' / 's after plural nouns that end in **s**.

8 Fill in the gaps. Use the words **men**, **women** and **children** with **'s**.

The .... toys are outside.

The .... skirts are here.

The .... ties aren't here.

9 Read what Splodge and Ruff say and answer the questions.

Splodge   *This is my comic.*
Ruff   *And this is your book.*

Who owns the comic? ....

Who owns the book? ....

10 Fill in the gaps. Use possessive pronouns (**mine**, **yours**, **his** etc).

This is my toy. It's ....

That's your dog. It's ....

This is his ink. It's ....

This is her doll. It's ....

This is our house. It's ....

This is their car. It's ....

REVISION 2 – quantifiers

1 Look at the nouns below. Are they nouns you can count or nouns you can't count? Tick the correct boxes.

	I can count	I can't count
eggs	☐	☐
milk	☐	☐
bread	☐	☐
tomatoes	☐	☐
cheese	☐	☐
sugar	☐	☐
apples	☐	☐
sweets	☐	☐
water	☐	☐
bananas	☐	☐

2 Read the examples and finish the rules.

I've got a pear and an apple.
I've got two pears and six apples.

Use .... and .... when there's one thing.

Use a .... when there's more than one thing and the things are easy to count.

3 Read what Splodge says and tick the correct boxes.

I've got some eggs and some milk.

Do you know how many eggs Splodge has got?
Yes ☐   No ☐

Do you know how much milk Splodge has got?
Yes ☐   No ☐

What kind of nouns do you use with **some**?
Nouns you can count   ☐
Nouns you can't count   ☐

4 Fill in the gaps. Use **a**, **an** or **some**.

He's eating .... orange.

He wants .... milk.

Have you got .... banana?

There are .... biscuits here.

5 Read the examples and cross out the wrong word.

Have we got any crisps?
Is there any lemonade?

Use **some** / **any** with all nouns to ask questions.

6 Read the examples and finish the rule.

We haven't got any bread.
There aren't any sweets.

Use **any** with all nouns in

positive / negative sentences.

7 Read the examples and tick the correct boxes.

How many biscuits are there?
How much bread is there?

how many is for nouns …
you can count.   ☐
you can't count.   ☐

how much is for nouns …
you can count.   ☐
you can't count.   ☐

8 Fill in the gaps.
Use **some**, **any**, **many** or **much**.

There isn't .... water.

How .... sweets are there?

There are .... pens here.

How .... cheese is there?

Nouns

1 Tick (✔) the correct box.

Look at the last picture. What's Milly looking at?
A telephone ☐   A television ☐

G GRAMMAR

A

Nouns are words for people, animals, things and places.

> *a boy, Snapper, a tiger, a table, London, Africa*
>
> *Mo has got a sister.*   *This is my book.*
> *Snapper is a crocodile.*   *London is in England.*

2 Look round the room. Write four nouns that you can see.

▶

....

....

....

....

B

You can count most nouns.

One (Singular)	Two or more (Plural)
a banana	*three bananas*
a crocodile	*ten crocodiles*
an orange	*oranges*
a boy	*boys*
a house	*houses*

3 Put the nouns in the correct list.

cats ✔   a book ✔   a tiger   chairs
five boys   a comic   two elephants
an egg

One	Two or more
▶ *a book*	*cats*
....	....
....	....
....	....

C

Use a singular verb with one, and a plural verb with two or more.

*The boy **is** naughty.*   *Oranges **are** nice.*
*A bicycle **has** got two wheels.*   *Sweets **taste** good.*

4 Write four sentences.
Use words from each box.

The cat		clever.
Dogs		big.
The school	is	small.
My friend	are	friendly.
My friends		fat.

▶ The cat is fat. ....

....

....

....

....

D

Be careful! You can't count these nouns.
Learn them.

water	NOT	~~waters~~	*meat*	NOT	~~meats~~
honey	NOT	~~honeys~~	*milk*	NOT	~~milks~~
bread	NOT	~~breads~~	*rice*	NOT	~~rices~~
cheese	NOT	~~cheeses~~	*juice*	NOT	~~juices~~

5 Circle the nouns you can't count.

```
r i c e s a n d w i c h e s p e a r s x
o n i o n s x n d a p r b r e a d r o
r a t h a u s m i c e n a f p l i o q s a
c h e e s e j u n i p e r m a t l o c k
g o r g n j k w s m u f f i s f i v e w
u f l e t w a t e r b m e a t r a i s q s
i n s m i l k r a b i d o g s h o n e y
```

E

Always use a singular verb with nouns you can't count.

*Honey **is** sweet.*
*Apple juice **tastes** nice.*

6 Write sentences. Use a singular verb.

▶ Honey / be / sweet

Honey is sweet. ....

1 Milk / be / white

....

2 Water / be / wet

....

3 Cheese / taste / good

....

4 Orange juice / taste / nice

....

F

Some nouns are names of people, places, days and months. Always use a capital letter.

Snapper, John, Paris, Cairo, Tuesday, June

Snapper is going to Ankara on Thursday.
Cairo is the capital of Egypt.
June comes after May.

7 Circle the mistakes.

People	**Places**	**Days and months**
▶ ⓢnapper	5 Egypt	10 june
1 John	6 cairo	11 March
2 milly	7 Athens	12 thursday
3 Richard	8 Rome	13 august
4 mabel	9 paris	14 Monday

PRACTICE

8

a Circle all the nouns you can see in the picture.

b Work with a partner. How many nouns can you think of which start with these letters? Take turns to say a noun each.

T ✔   **A**   **M**   **C**

▶ Partner A   *A tree.*
   Partner B   *Tokyo.*
   Partner A   *A tiger.*
   Partner B   *Thomas.*

9

a Look at the pictures. Colour the box if you can count the noun. Don't colour the box if you can't count the noun.

b Swap books with a partner. Have you both coloured the same boxes?

How many nouns can you count? ....

How many nouns can't you count? ....

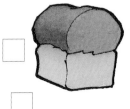

10

a Cross out the wrong verbs. Be careful!

Snapper Apples ► is/are my favourite fruit. And apple juice (1) are/is my favourite drink.

Mo Yuck! I (2) like/likes bananas. Chocolate milkshakes (3) is/are my favourite drink. What do you like, Milly?

Milly I think cherries (4) is/are the best fruit. Milk (5) are/is my favourite drink, but orange juice (6) is/are nice, too.

Snapper What do you like eating, Mo?

Mo Sweets and biscuits (7) are/is delicious. Honey sandwiches (8) is/are good. My friend (9) eat/eats egg and jam sandwiches.

Milly That's horrible! What drink does he like?

Mo He loves apple juice but he says lettuce juice (10) tastes/taste best.

Snapper Mo, please don't invite him here!

b Work with a partner. Look at the nouns below. Take turns to say a sentence about each one.

milk   bread   biscuits   apples
butter   meat   tomatoes   water
milkshakes   sweets

► Partner A   *Milk is nice.* OR *My sister likes milk.*
  Partner B   *I like bread.* OR *Bread is good.*

11

a Mo is writing about his holiday. There are lots of mistakes! Circle all the mistakes you can find.

In (June I'm going to france.
Snapper and Milly are coming
with me. june is a good month
because it's hot. France are a
big country. First, we is going
to paris. It's a large city.
Every thursday there are a
market. Then we're going to
the seaside. snapper are
packing his suitcase already!

Snapper

b Now write the words correctly.

In ► June............ I'm going to ....
Snapper and Milly are coming with me.

.... is a good month because it's

hot. France .... a big country.

First, we .... going to ....

It's a large city. Every .... there

.... a market. Then we're going to the

seaside. .... packing his

suitcase already!

12 Ask your teacher if you can play a class game. Play the game like this:

► Pupil A   *Mo wants a banana.*
  Pupil B   *Mo wants a banana and three cakes.*
  Pupil C   *Mo wants a banana, three cakes and a bicycle.*
  Pupil D   *Mo wants a banana, three cakes, a bicycle and two comics.*

Subject and object pronouns

> Where's Ruff?
> I can't find **him**.

1 Tick (✔) the correct boxes.

- Who's hiding?
  Tumble ☐   Ruff ☐

- Who's looking for Ruff?
  Splodge ☐   Mabel ☐

GRAMMAR

REMEMBER!

Sentences often have a subject, a verb and an object.

Subject	Verb	Object
Splodge	*can't find*	*Ruff.*
Tumble	*is reading*	*a book.*
Splodge	*is eating*	*a mud pie.*
Ruff	*invents*	*machines.*

See Chapter 38.

2 Circle the subjects and objects.
How many are there?

(Splodge) is looking for Ruff. Splodge can't find Ruff. Ruff is watching Splodge. Tumble is reading a book. Mildred is making cakes. Mabel is talking to her tortoise. Splodge's rabbit is eating a carrot. Now Splodge can see Ruff!

There are .... subjects.

There are .... objects.

A

Subject pronouns replace subject nouns. Look:

Subject nouns		Subject pronouns
Ruff is funny.	→	*He's funny.*
Tumble is reading.	→	*He's reading.*
Mildred is cooking.	→	*She's cooking.*
Mabel is talking.	→	*She's talking.*
Splodge and Ruff like games.	→	*They like games.*

3 Which sentences mean the same? Draw lines.

▶ Splodge is playing.

1 Mabel and Mildred are cooking.

2 Mabel likes tortoises.

3 Splodge eats mud pies.

4 Tumble and Ruff love Splodge.

They love Splodge.

She likes tortoises.

He eats mud pies.

They're cooking.

He's playing.

B

These are subject pronouns.

I	*I like Splodge.*
you	*He eats mud pies.*
he	*They're very good.*
she	
it	
we	
you	
they	

4 Replace the subject nouns with subject pronouns.

▶ Splodge is funny.   He..........'s funny.

1 Mildred is making cakes.   ....'s making cakes.

2 Tumble reads newspapers.   .... reads newspapers.

3 Ruff and Splodge are playing.   ....'re playing.

4 Mud pies are very good.   ....'re very good.

C

Object pronouns replace object nouns.

Object nouns		Object pronouns
Splodge likes **Ruff**.	→	*Splodge likes **him**.*
Ruff likes **chocolate**.	→	*Ruff likes **it**.*
Tumble talks to **Mabel**.	→	*Tumble talks to **her**.*
Splodge eats **mud pies**.	→	*Splodge eats **them**.*

5 Circle the object pronouns.

▶ Splodge is looking for Ruff. He can't find (him).

1 Ruff is hiding. He doesn't want Splodge to find him.

2 Tumble is reading a book. He's enjoying it.

3 Mildred is making cakes. Splodge is eating them.

4 Mabel is talking to her tortoise. It isn't listening to her.

D

These are object pronouns.

me	*I like **him**.*
you	*Mabel is talking to **her**.*
him	*Splodge eats **them**.*
her	
it	
us	
you	
them	

6 Replace the object nouns with object pronouns.

▶ Tumble reads newspapers.　　　　He reads *them.*................

1 Mildred is making the cake.　　　Mildred is making ....

2 Splodge can't see Ruff.　　　　　Splodge can't see ....

3 Mabel likes Ruff and Tumble.　　Mabel likes ....

4 Mabel is helping Mildred.　　　　Mabel is helping ....

P PRACTICE

7

a Fill in the table.

Subject pronoun	Object pronoun
I	me
she	
	it
we	
	them

b Write four sentences using a subject pronoun and four sentences using an object pronoun.

▶ I like Splodge.................................

　 Tumble talks to him.........................

　 ....

　 ....

　 ....

　 ....

　 ....

　 ....

　 ....

8

a What do you like? Read the questionnaire. Put a tick (✔) or a cross (✗) in the boxes.

chocolate biscuits	☐	the summer	☐
Splodge	☐	English lessons	☐
your neighbour	☐	your best friend	☐
your school	☐	holidays	☐
spiders	☐	dogs	☐
cartoons	☐	football	☐
your doctor	☐	television	☐
Mabel	☐	mud pies	☐
rain	☐	milkshakes	☐

b Now work with a partner. Take turns to ask and answer the questions. Use **I** and object pronouns.

▶ Partner A　*Do you like chocolate biscuits?*
　 Partner B　*Yes, I like them.* OR
　　　　　　 No, I don't like them.

　 Partner B　*Do you like the summer?*
　 Partner A　*Yes, I like it.* OR *No, I don't like it.*

c Swap books with a partner. Take turns to tell the class two things that your partner likes and doesn't like.

▶ Pupil A　*She likes chocolate biscuits but she doesn't like spiders.*
　 Pupil B　*He likes mud pies but he doesn't like his neighbour.*
　 Pupil C　*She likes football but she doesn't like rain.*

9

a Read the conversation. Fill in the gaps.
   Use a subject or object pronoun.

Mildred Splodge, where are ▶ you........? I'm

looking for (1) ....

Mabel Mildred and I are going out. (2) ....'re going

shopping. Do (3) .... want to come with (4) .... ?

Splodge Yes, please. Can we go to the toyshop? (5) ....

love toys and I want to buy a present for Ruff. He's angry

with (6) ....

Mildred Yes, ask Tumble to give (7) .... some money.

Splodge Can you give (8) .... some money, Tumble?

(9) .... want to go shopping.

Tumble Sorry, Splodge. (10) .... haven't got any money.

Why don't (11) .... ask Ruff to give (12) ....

some money? (13) ....'s always got money.

Splodge I don't want to ask (14) .... He's angry

with me because there's glue in his shoes.

Mabel Why is there glue in his shoes?

Splodge What a silly question! Because I put glue in his shoes.

b Now read the questions and complete
   the answers.

▶ Is Mabel going shopping with Ruff?
   No, she........ isn't.

1 Who's she going shopping with?
   ....'s going with Mildred.

2 Does Splodge want to go with them?
   Yes, ... does.

3 Which shop are they going to?
   ....'re going to the toyshop.

4 Does Splodge like toys? Yes, ... does.

5 What does Splodge ask Tumble for?
   He asks .... for some money.

6 Has Tumble got any money?
   No, ... hasn't.

7 What does Splodge want to buy?
   .... wants to buy a present for Ruff.

8 Why doesn't he want to ask Ruff for money?
   Because Ruff is angry with ....

10 Take turns to ask one question each round the
   class. Ask about likes and dislikes. The person
   sitting next to you answers your question.
   Play the game like this:

▶ Teacher *Do you like television?*
   Pupil A *Yes, I like it. Do you like Fizzy Ink?*
   Pupil B *No, I don't like it. Do you like snakes?*
   Pupil C *Yes, I like them. Do you like Mickey Mouse?*
   Pupil D *Yes, I like him. Do you like bananas?*

10 Plurals

I've got a dog. Ruff has got dog, dog. Tumble has got dog, dog, dog.

No, Splodge, listen! You've got a dog. Ruff has got two **dogs**. I've got three **dogs**. It's easy!

1 Tick (✔) the correct box.

Ruff has got dog, dog. ☐
Ruff has got two dogs. ☐

G GRAMMAR

REMEMBER!

Nouns are words for people, animals, things and places.

*a **girl**, a **crocodile**, a **table**, **Rome***

See Chapter 8.

2 Write four more nouns.

▶ a house ....
....
....
....

A

Add **s** to most nouns.

a dog → *two dog**s***
a cat → *cat**s***
a boy → *four boys*
a girl → *girl**s***

3 Make the words plural.

▶ a dog   dogs...

1 a flower   ....

2 the tree   ....

3 a book   ....

4 the horse   ....

B

Add **es** to nouns ending in **o**, **x**, **s**, **sh** or **ch**.

a potato	→	*three potatoes*
a fox	→	*foxes*
a dress	→	*three dresses*
a toothbrush	→	*toothbrushes*
a watch	→	*six watches*

4 Look at the plurals below.
Find them in the puzzle.

toothbrushes ✔ beaches brushes
buses bushes classes dishes
dresses foxes hairbrushes matches
potatoes tomatoes watches

```
t o o t h b r u s h e s p l o d g e b u s e s p o t a t o e s
s m u f f d r e s s e s y o d e l n o t h b r u s h e s d a s
h t o m a t o e s g u s h f o x e s c r a n m e r l a t i n
b u s h e s y r t u m b l e m a n m o o n k h i n e t l
n b e a h a i r b r u s h e s n u t t y d i s h e s c l a s s e s
r a t i b i l l e d f l a t y p u s w a t c h e s a n d t h i
m a t c h e s a l s o b e a c h e s r i d l e y g o r g e w
```

REMEMBER!

These are consonants:

**b, c, d, f, g, h, j, k, l, m, n,
p, q, r, s, t, v, w, x, y, z**

See Chapter 38.

5 Circle the consonants.

C

If nouns end in a consonant + **y**, change **y** to **i**
and add **es**.

a baby	→	*two babies*
the lady	→	*the ladies*
a dictionary	→	*dictionaries*

6 Fill in the gaps. Use the plural of the
words below.

city ✔ body story party baby

▶ Mabel doesn't like cities...........

1 Splodges have small ....

2 Tumble tells good ....

3 Splodge loves going to ....

4 Splodge doesn't like ....

D

Be careful! Learn these plurals.

a person	→	*two **people***
the child	→	*the **children***
my tooth	→	*my **teeth***
a man	→	*five **men***
a woman	→	*nine **women***
my foot	→	*my **feet***

7 Write the plurals.

▶ There's a woman in the shop.

There are two women......... in the shop.

1 My tooth hurts.

My .... hurt.

2 I can see a child in the park.

I can see three .... in the park.

3 Splodge is standing on Mabel's foot.

Splodge is standing on Mabel's ....

4 There's a man in that car.

There are four .... in that car.

PRACTICE

8

a Tumble and Ruff are going shopping. Fill in the gaps. Use plurals.

Tumble What do we need to buy for the party?

Ruff We need ▶ _flowers_ .... (flower) and

(1) .... (balloon).

Tumble No, stupid! You can't eat balloons. What food

do we need?

Ruff (2) .... (crisp) and

(3) .... (peanut).

Tumble Let's buy twelve (4) .... (melon).

Ruff We can have burgers and (5) .... (chip).

Tumble With (6) .... (vegetable).

Let's buy twenty (7) .... (burger),

(8) .... (potato), (9) .... (carrot)

and (10) .... (pea).

Ruff For my *Starlight Surprise* pudding I need

(11) .... (apple), (12) .... (orange),

(13) .... (banana), (14) .... (peach),

(15) .... (cherry) and two pencils.

Tumble Pencils? Why do you need pencils?

Ruff I can't tell you. It's a surprise.

b Work with a partner. Write what you think Splodge needs to make this recipe.

SPLODGE'S STRAWBERRY SNOW

▶ _two eggs, three bananas,_ ....

....

....

....

....

....

Now read your list to the class.

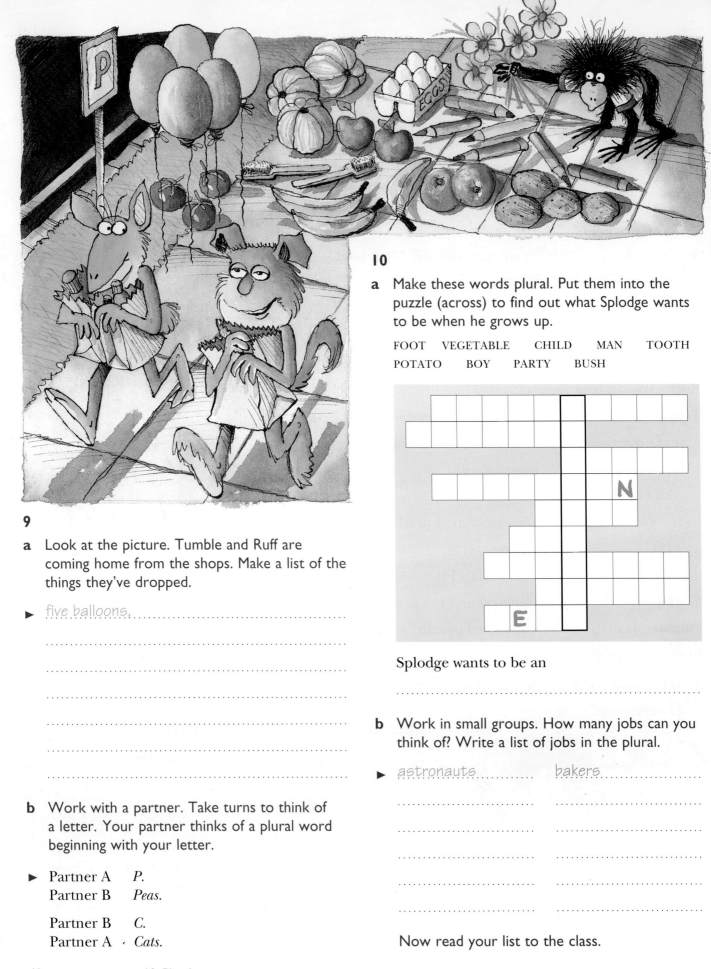

9

a Look at the picture. Tumble and Ruff are coming home from the shops. Make a list of the things they've dropped.

▶ five balloons,

....

....

....

....

....

....

b Work with a partner. Take turns to think of a letter. Your partner thinks of a plural word beginning with your letter.

▶ Partner A   *P.*
  Partner B   *Peas.*

  Partner B   *C.*
  Partner A ⸳ *Cats.*

10

a Make these words plural. Put them into the puzzle (across) to find out what Splodge wants to be when he grows up.

FOOT   VEGETABLE   CHILD   MAN   TOOTH
POTATO   BOY   PARTY   BUSH

Splodge wants to be an

....

b Work in small groups. How many jobs can you think of? Write a list of jobs in the plural.

▶ astronauts   bakers

....

....

....

....

....

Now read your list to the class.

11

a Read the passage. Circle all the plurals you can find.

Splodge, Ruff and Tumble love (parties.) Today all their friends are coming to the house. There are flowers on the table. Ruff is washing the dishes and glasses. Tumble is making a fruit salad. He's got apples, cherries, strawberries and a melon. Splodge is cooking the burgers and the vegetables. He's got carrots, peas and potatoes. There are presents for everyone. People like presents. Splodge has got special presents for the children.

b Now answer the questions.

▶ What do Splodge, Ruff and Tumble love?

They love *parties*.....................

1 Who's coming to the house today?

.... are coming

to the house.

2 What's on the table?

There are .... on the table.

3 What's Ruff washing?

He's washing ....

....

4 What has Tumble got for his fruit salad?

He's got ....

....

5 What's Splodge cooking?

He's cooking ....

....

12

a Read the story.

Splodge's neighbour Mabel likes shopping. She goes to the greengrocer's, the post office, the newsagent's and the supermarket. Mabel is strange. She buys two of everything. Today she wants to buy two pencils … Oh, dear! Mabel can't find her list.

b Now work with a partner. Write Mabel's list. What do you think she wants to buy? Remember! Two of everything.

▶ *two apples* ....

....

....

....

....

c Swap books with two other pupils. Read their lists to the class.

13 Ask your teacher if you can play 'In Splodge's house'. Play the game like this:

▶ Pupil A   *In Splodge's house I see three children.*
  Pupil B   *In Splodge's house I see three children and two rabbits.*
  Pupil C   *In Splodge's house I see three children, two rabbits and …*

REVISION 3 – nouns; subject pronouns; object pronouns

1 Circle the nouns.

Snapper is a crocodile and Mo is a boy. They like eating crisps and cheese. They also like living in England.

2 Tick the correct boxes.

	Singular	Plural
a toy	☐	☐
houses	☐	☐
friends	☐	☐
a dog	☐	☐
a tree	☐	☐
apples	☐	☐
a school	☐	☐
biscuits	☐	☐
books	☐	☐
a computer	☐	☐

3 Read the examples and finish the rule.

This apple is green.
These apples are green.

Singular nouns have a

.... verb.

Plural nouns have a

.... verb.

4 Circle the nouns you can't count.

Mo loves biscuits, sweets, cheese and milk.
He hates lettuce, tea and coffee.

5 Read the examples and tick the correct box.

Is there lemonade in the fridge?
Honey tastes very sweet.

Use a singular verb with nouns
you can't count. ☐

Use a plural verb with nouns
you can't count. ☐

6 Circle the subjects and underline the objects of these sentences.

Snapper loves fishing.

Mo eats sweets every day.

7 Read the sentence and answer the questions.

Mo loves football. He plays it a lot.

Who's 'He'? ....

What's 'it'? ....

8 Fill in the object pronouns.

Subject pronoun	Object pronoun
I	
you	
he	
she	
it	
we	
you	
they	

9 Fill the gaps. Use subject and object pronouns.

Milly loves drinking milkshakes.

.... drinks a lot of ....

Mo likes playing tennis. .... plays

.... every Saturday.

11 Adjectives

Tumble, help!
It's a !?!?!? mouse!

No, Splodge.
It's a **big** mouse. You
need an adjective!

An adjective?
I need a mousetrap.

I Tick (✔) the correct box.

What's big?   Splodge ☐   The mouse ☐

REMEMBER!

These are nouns.

a **mouse**, a **table**, a **flower**, **Richard**,
Splodge, a **chair**, an **apple**, **London**

See Chapter 8.

2 Write four more nouns.

....

....

A

Adjectives tell you more about nouns.

	Noun
It's a	mouse.

	Adjective	**Noun**
It's a	**big**	*mouse.*

3 Use some of the words in the two lists below
to complete the sentences.

Adjectives
big   brown   small   young   good   bad
nice   clever   funny   hot   cold   beautiful

Nouns
teacher   boy   girl   mouse   day   country
town   man   woman   book   elephant   dog

▶ He's a clever boy. ....

  She's a good teacher. ....

  It's a nice day. ....

1 She's a ....

2 It's a ....

3 He's a ....

4 She's a ....

B

Adjectives can go before a noun.

	Adjective	Noun
It's a	**big**	mouse.

4 Put the adjective in the correct place.

▶ It's a rabbit. (small) *It's a small rabbit.*

1 It's a mouse. (big) ....

2 These are birds. (noisy) ....

3 It's a lion. (sleepy) ....

4 It's a monkey. (young) ....

C

Adjectives can go after the verb **be**.

Noun	Verb	Adjective
The	mouse	is	**big**.

5 Write sentences using the words below.
Use the correct form of **be**.

▶ The / school / big — *The school is big.*

The / dog / dirty — *The dog is dirty.*

I / sleepy — *I'm sleepy.*

1 Our / teacher / nice ....

2 I / hungry ....

3 Splodge / funny ....

4 The / mouse / brown ....

red rabbit the small banana interesting dangerous bad kangaroo zoo fat tree sun long giraffe old happy green sad dirty tiger a heavy and difficult Splodge clever short easy school he thin talk yellow worm cat big

P PRACTICE

6 Splodge is looking for adjectives.
How many can you see? Circle them.
Now write sentences using ten of the
adjectives. Put the adjective before the noun.

▶ *This is a big school.*

....

....

....

....

....

....

....

....

....

....

7 Rewrite the sentences. Put the adjective after the verb **be**.

▶ This is a brown bear.   This bear is brown.

1 These are noisy monkeys.   ....

2 This is a hungry tiger.   ....

3 This is a sleepy crocodile.   ....

4 These are dirty dogs.   ....

5 These are beautiful birds.   ....

6 This is an angry lion.   ....

7 This is a small mouse.   ....

8 This is a dangerous spider.   ....

9 These are thirsty giraffes.   ....

10 This is a grey elephant.   ....

8

a Splodge is talking about a strange animal.
Draw it in the space on the right.

'It's got a large body. It's got long legs and
small feet. It's got green eyes and a short nose.
It's got yellow fur and big ears. It's got a long,
thin neck. It's got a large mouth and sharp,
white teeth. It's eating a green plant.'

b Work with a partner. Take turns to tell your
partner what to draw.

▶ Partner A   *Draw a big house. It's got a yellow
                door and small windows.*

  Partner B   *Draw a fish. It's got red eyes and
                a long tail.*

9

a Match the sentences.

► Splodge's face isn't clean.   I'm hot.

1 I'm not cold.   They're small.

2 That bird isn't ugly.   We're noisy.

3 We aren't quiet.   He's young.

4 Tumble isn't old.   It's beautiful.

5 Mice aren't big.   It's dirty.

---

6 I'm not sad.   She's nice.

7 You aren't short.   He's clever.

8 Splodge isn't stupid.   I'm happy.

9 Hippos aren't thin.   You're tall.

10 Mabel isn't nasty.   They're fat.

b Work in two teams. Team A, say an adjective. Team B, make a sentence using the adjective. Score a point for each correct sentence.

► Team A   *Beautiful.*
   Team B   *It's a beautiful day!*

   Team B   *Tall.*
   Team A   *Giraffes are tall.*

10 Work with a partner. Take turns to think of an animal, a person or an object. Try to describe it to your partner. Play the game like this:

► Partner A   *It's black and white.*
   Partner B   *Is it a newspaper?*
   Partner A   *No. It's got a big body and short ears.*
   Partner B   *Is it a zebra?*
   Partner A   *Yes!*

11 Write a story. Use some words from the list to help you.

big   dangerous   tall   black   old   hat
castle   tiger   forest   garden   tree

► *In the big castle there's an old man. He's very tall. He wears a black hat.*

Start your story like this:

In the dark forest there's ....

....

....

....

....

....

....

....

....

Now read your story to the class.

Adverbs of manner

Who are you?

I'm an Adverb.
I work **hard** all day, and
I do everything **quickly**.

Oh, good. Come
and tidy my room.

I Tick (✔) the correct box.

The Adverb does everything slowly.
True ☐   False ☐

GRAMMAR

REMEMBER!

Adjectives tell you more about nouns.

*Splodge is **funny**.*   *It's a **big** dog.*

See Chapter 11.

2 Circle the adjectives.

Splodge is funny. He's very happy. He likes
Ruff and Tumble. They're nice. They all live
together in a small town called Wibble. It's got
interesting shops, a large park and a good
school. In the park there are tall trees and
there's a big playground.

He eats messily.

A

Adverbs of manner tell you more about verbs.

Noun	Verb
Splodge	eats.
Ruff	cooks.

Noun	Verb	Adverb
Splodge	*eats*	**quickly**.
Ruff	*cooks*	**badly**.

3 Circle the verbs and underline the adverbs.

Ruff   You play music loudly. You shout noisily

and you sing badly.

Splodge   No, I don't! Tumble sings badly.

I sing beautifully. And I always behave nicely.

Ruff   That's not true! Go and do your

homework in your bedroom. And do it quietly

and carefully, please.

Splodge   Oh, no! I hate homework.

B

It's easy to make an adverb. Adjective + **ly**.

Adjective		Adverb
beautiful	→	*beautifully*
bad	→	*badly*
quick	→	*quickly*

*He sings **badly**.*   *I sing **beautifully**.*

4 Turn these adjectives into adverbs.

► beautiful   *beautifully*

1 careful   ....

2 nice   ....

3 quiet   ....

4 slow   ....

C

If the adjective ends in **y**, change **y** to **i** and add **ly**.

Adjective		Adverb
noisy	→	*noisily*
easy	→	*easily*

*Splodge shouts **noisily**.*
*We can do our homework **easily**.*

5 Finish the sentences. Use an adverb.

► Ruff is shouting at Splodge .angrily.. (angry)

1 Ruff can do Maths .... (easy)

2 Ruff is laughing .... (happy)

3 Splodge eats very...................... (messy)

4 Splodge sings .... (noisy)

D

Be careful! Learn these.

Adjective		Adverb
good	→	*well*
fast	→	*fast*
hard	→	*hard*

*Splodge cooks mud pies **well**.*   *Ruff runs **fast**.*

6 Read the sentences. Tick the correct word.

► Splodge gets bad marks at school because he

doesn't work ...   messy. ☐   hard. ☑

1 Ruff doesn't like going in Mildred's car

because she drives very ...   fast. ☐   happy. ☐

2 Splodge's English teacher says, 'Splodge, you

must work ...   clever.' ☐   hard.' ☐

3 Splodge can't understand what Mabel says.

She talks very ...   fast. ☐   bad. ☐

4 Tumble is a good storyteller. He tells stories

very ...   stupid. ☐   well. ☐

7

a Splodge is talking to the Adverb. Fill in the gaps.

Splodge Ruff says I must ask you questions

▶ ..politely........ (polite). How old are you?

Adverb I'm a hundred and three.

Splodge A hundred and three! That's old. Do you work

(1) .... (hard)?

Adverb Yes, I work very hard. I do things

(2) .... (quick). I can swim and run

(3) .... (good), too.

Splodge I can't run (4) .... (fast). I run very

(5) .... (slow). Can you do homework

(6) .... (easy)?

Adverb Yes, of course. I can do Maths, History and

English easily. I write very (7) .... (careful)

and (8) .... (slow). I always get good marks.

Splodge Good. You can do my homework. Can you

put toys in the toy box (9) .... (quick)?

Adverb Yes, it's easy. I'm very tidy.

Splodge What do you do (10) .... (bad)?

Adverb Nothing. I do everything perfectly.

b Work with a partner. Take turns to ask and answer five questions. Use some of the words in the lists below.

eat	easily
run	slowly
swim	quickly
dance	carefully
read	well
walk	fast
do homework	badly
write	messily
play football	tidily
shout	loudly
do Maths	hard
work	correctly
ride a bicycle	beautifully

▶ Partner A *What do you do easily?*
Partner B *I do Maths easily.*
What do you do badly?
Partner A *I write badly.*

12 Adverbs of manner   **49**

8 Write how these people and animals do things. Use adverbs.

► A painter paints beautifully......... (beautiful)

1 Splodge learns .... (quick)

2 A footballer plays football .... (good)

3 A baby eats .... (messy)

4 Mabel drives her car .... (fast)

5 A tortoise walks .... (slow)

6 Mildred cooks mud pies .... (bad)

7 Ruff does Maths .... (easy)

8 An opera singer sings .... (noisy)

9 A cat moves .... (quiet)

10 Splodge talks.............................. (loud)

9 Splodge is writing a letter to Uncle Badpaw but he doesn't know many adverbs. Help him fill in the gaps. Make the adjectives below into adverbs.

good ✔   perfect ✔   loud   noisy
quiet   hard   neat   slow   messy
fast   bad   good

10 Work with a partner. Take turns to make and answer questions. Use words from the two lists.

read English   paint   swim   sing
play an instrument   run   learn facts
cook   write letters   eat   do Maths
speak another language

easily   beautifully   noisily   neatly
quickly   well   badly   loudly   fast
perfectly   messily   correctly

► Partner A   *Can you read English easily?*
  Partner B   *Yes, I can. Can you paint beautifully?*
  Partner A   *No, I can't.*

11 Ask your teacher if you can play a class game. Listen very carefully to what your friends say! Play the game like this:

► Pupil A   *Splodge eats messily.*
  Pupil B   *Splodge eats messily and dances well.*
  Pupil C   *Splodge eats messily, dances well and sings loudly.*
  Pupil D   *Splodge eats messily, dances well, sings loudly and runs slowly.*

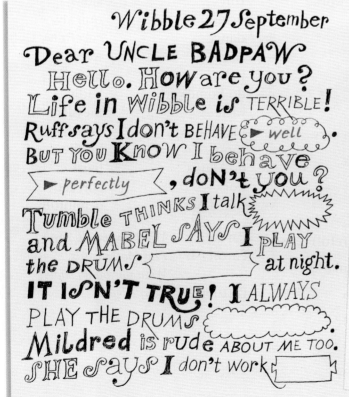

Adverbs of frequency

WHY DO DUCKS **ALWAYS** FLY TO OTHER COUNTRIES IN THE WINTER, SNAPPER?

THEY FLY BECAUSE IT'S TOO FAR TO WALK, SILLY.

?

YOU **NEVER** GIVE ME THE RIGHT ANSWER!

1 Tick (✔) the correct box.

Ducks go to other countries in the winter.
How do they get there?
They walk. ☐   They fly. ☐

GRAMMAR

REMEMBER!

The present simple is to talk about things that you do again and again.

*I **go** to school.*
*He **has** breakfast at eight o'clock.*
*Ducks always **fly** away in the winter.*

See Chapter 18.

2 Write four things that you do every day.

▶ I go to school. . . . .

. . . .

. . . .

. . . .

. . . .

A

Adverbs of frequency tell you *when* something happens.
Use them with the present simple.

Noun	Verb
Ducks	fly.
Snapper	eats ice cream.
Mo	walks to school.

Noun	Adverb	Verb
Ducks	*always*	*fly away in the winter.* = every winter
Snapper	*never*	*eats ice cream.* = He doesn't eat ice cream.
Mo	*usually*	*walks to school.* = most days but not every day

3 What do these sentences mean? Tick the correct boxes.

1 Snapper **always** gets up at six o'clock.
   He gets up at six every day. ☐   He doesn't get up at six. ☐
2 Mo **never** does his homework.
   He does his homework. ☐   He doesn't do his homework. ☐

B

always = all the time; **never** = not at all
Look at the table to see what the other words mean.

always	=	■ ■ ■ ■ ■ ■ ■
usually	=	■ ■ ■ ■ ■ ■ □
often	=	■ □ ■ ■ ■ ■ □
sometimes	=	□ □ □ ■ □ □ ■
rarely	=	■ □ □ □ □ □ □
never	=	□ □ □ □ □ □ □

4 Write four sentences. Use some of the words below if you need help.

go swimming   brush my teeth   miss school
eat mud pies   talk in class   walk to school
ride my bicycle   read a book   drink milk
play with friends   stand on my head

► Snapper rarely *eats lettuce.* ....

I sometimes ....

I often ....

I never ....

I usually ....

C

You can put these adverbs *before* all full verbs.

*I **always get up** at six o'clock.*
*Snapper **sometimes helps** Mo to do his homework.*
*We **never eat** chocolate.*
*They **usually go** swimming on Thursdays.*

5 Make four sentences. Use a verb and an adverb in each sentence.

play   dance   always   rarely
read   listen   usually   never
swim   watch   often   sometimes
sing   eat

► *Mo never reads a Maths book.*

I often sing a song. ....

....

....

....

....

D

You can also put these adverbs *after* be.

*I'm **always** happy.*
*Mo **is usually** hungry.*
*We're **often** busy.*
*Mo and Snapper **are never** bored.*

6 Put the words in the correct order.

► unhappy.   never   Snapper   is

Snapper is never unhappy. ....

1 is   sometimes   Mo   naughty.

....

2 is   always   hungry.   Snapper

....

3 Mo's mum   is   tired.   often

....

4 is   Milly   usually   happy.

....

PRACTICE

7

a Put the adverbs in the correct places. Be careful!

► Dogs bark at night. (often)
  Dogs often bark at night.

1 Birds are noisy. (often)
  ....

2 Giraffes are tall. (always)
  ....

3 Cats go out at night. (usually)
  ....

4 Bears climb trees. (sometimes)
  ....

5 Rabbits have long ears. (always)
  ....

6 Monkeys are very clever. (usually)
  ....

7 Snakes bite people. (sometimes)
  ....

8 Cats like water. (rarely)
  ....

9 Chickens fly. (never)
  ....

10 Ducks stand on one leg. (often)
  ....

b Work with a partner. Answer these questions. There are lots of possible answers.

► What animal sometimes has red eyes?
  A rabbit sometimes has red eyes.

  What animal always has a tail?
  A horse always has a tail.

1 What animal always lives near water?
  ....

2 What animal rarely moves fast?
  ....

3 What animal sometimes climbs trees?
  ....

4 What animal usually jumps?
  ....

5 What animal often eats grass?
  ....

c Now work with two more friends. Take turns to ask and answer the questions. Have your friends got the same answers as you?

► Pupil A   *What animal sometimes has red eyes?*
  Pupil C   *A rabbit sometimes has red eyes.*

  Pupil B   *What animal always has a tail?*
  Pupil D   *A horse always has a tail.*

8

a Write answers to the questions. Use an adverb.

How often do you … ?

▶ shout *I never shout.* ....

1 tell jokes ....

2 play football ....

3 buy sweets ....

4 go swimming ....

5 go to see a doctor ....
....

6 tell the truth ....

7 forget to do your homework ....
....

8 read a book ....

9 use a telephone ....
....

10 watch television ....
....

11 stand on one leg ....
....

12 go to another country ....
....

13 speak English ....

14 eat bananas ....
....

15 have a nice dream ....
....

b Swap books with a partner. Take turns to read your partner's answers to the class.

▶ Pupil A *George sometimes shouts.*
Pupil B *Maria often tells jokes.*

Pupil C *Richard never plays football.*
Pupil D *Ann rarely buys sweets.*

9 Look at the sentences below. Write new, true sentences using these adverbs: **never**, **always**, **often**, **sometimes**.

It's cold in winter. ✔
I'm friendly.
We have a lot of homework.
The sun is hot.
Rabbits speak.
Dogs bite people.
Birds sing.
The sky is green.
Ice is hot.
Tables have three legs.
I eat eggs.

▶ *It's often cold in winter.* ....

1 ....

2 ....

3 ....

4 ....

5 ....

6 ....

7 ....

8 ....

9 ....

10 ....

10 Ask your teacher if you can play this game. Take turns round the class to say a sentence each. Use an adverb in your sentence. Don't use the same adverb as the last pupil.

▶ Pupil A *Snapper always eats apples for breakfast.*
Pupil B *I'm usually asleep all day.*
Pupil C *We often play games in class.*
Pupil D *I sometimes fly to Mars.*

REVISION 4 – adjectives; adverbs

1 Read the sentences and answer the questions.

Splodge is funny.
The machine makes big biscuits.

Who's funny? ....

What's big? ....

2 Read the sentences and answer the questions.

That dog is friendly.
I've got a red car.

What do you know about the dog?

It's ....

What do you know about the car?

It's ....

3 Read the examples and tick the correct box.

Rabbits have got long ears.
This is a big mouse.

Adjectives tell you more about …
verbs. ☐   nouns. ☐

4 Read the examples and tick the correct box.

These are noisy parrots.
That's an interesting machine.

An adjective can go …
after a noun. ☐   before a noun. ☐

5 Read the examples and cross out the wrong word in the rule below.

The mouse is big.
Those parrots are noisy.

An adjective can go after / before the verb **be**.

6 Read the sentences and answer the questions.

Splodge eats messily.
Ruff reads quickly.

What does Splodge do messily?

He .... messily.

What does Ruff do quickly?

He .... quickly.

7 Read the examples and write the rule.

Mildred works hard.
Ruff sings badly.

Adverbs tell you more about

....

8 Make the adjectives into adverbs.

quick ....

bad ....

angry ....

easy ....

good ....

fast ....

9 Read the examples and tick the correct boxes.

He's always happy.
Mabel is sometimes angry.
I usually go to school at eight.
They often eat ice cream.

These adverbs go …
before the verb **be**. ☐
after the verb **be**. ☐

before other verbs. ☐
after other verbs. ☐

Be

> I'm Splodge. I'm funny. That's my rabbit. He's my friend. Rabbits **are** nice. They**'re** clever and ...

> Splodge! Shhhh! It's midnight.

I Tick (✔) the correct boxes.

- Is Splodge funny?   Yes ☐   No ☐

- Splodge thinks rabbits are ...   stupid. ☐   clever. ☐

GRAMMAR

A

be is to talk about yourself and other people, animals or things.

I'm a girl.	*I'm thin.*
She's a doctor.	*He's funny.*
It's a tiger.	*It's big.*
*They **aren't** doctors.*	*They **aren't** tall.*

2 Write two things about yourself and two things about someone you know.

▶ I'm tall.

My mother is a teacher.

....

....

....

....

B

Make **be** like this:

Positive +

I**'m**
you**'re**
he**'s**
she**'s**
it**'s**
we**'re**
you**'re**
they**'re**

See page 170.

3 Write four sentences. Use the words below to help you.

girls ✔   a boy   happy
my friend   a cat

► We're girls. ....

....

....

....

....

C

Make the negative of **be** like this:

Negative –

I**'m not**
you **aren't**
he **isn't**
she **isn't**
it **isn't**
we **aren't**
you **aren't**
they **aren't**

See page 170.

4 Make the sentences negative.

► Splodge is naughty.   Splodge isn't naughty. ....

They're doctors.   They aren't doctors. ....

1 It's a good film.   ....

2 We're at school.   ....

3 She's tall.   ....

4 I'm hungry.   ....

D

Question	Short answer		
Am I?	Yes, I **am**.	OR	No, I**'m not**.
Are you?	Yes, you **are**.	OR	No, you **aren't**.
Is he?	Yes, he **is**.	OR	No, he **isn't**.
Is she?	Yes, she **is**.	OR	No, she **isn't**.
Is it?	Yes, it **is**.	OR	No, it **isn't**.
Are we?	Yes, we **are**.	OR	No, we **aren't**.
Are you?	Yes, you **are**.	OR	No, you **aren't**.
Are they?	Yes, they **are**.	OR	No, they **aren't**.

5

a Put the words in the correct order.

► tall?   Are   you   Are you tall? ....

1 a boy?   Are   you   ....

2 a girl?   you   Are   ....

b Work with a partner. Take turns to ask and answer the two questions. Use **yes, I am** or **no, I'm not**.

6 Fill in the table. Use the correct form of **be**.

Positive +	Negative –	Question
	I'm not	
		Are you?
he's		
	she isn't	
		Is it?
we're		
	you aren't	
		Are they?

7

a Write sentences. Use the correct form of **be**.

► I / young
  I'm young.

1 She / clever

2 You / not old

3 You / sleepy

4 We / not noisy

5 You / not tall

6 It / cold

7 They / funny

8 He / not tired

9 You / beautiful

10 He / nice

11 We / happy

12 I / not sad

13 She / angry

14 They / untidy

b Write five questions to ask a friend.

► Is your brother tall?

c Now work with a partner. Take turns to ask and answer your questions.

► Partner A *Is your brother tall?*
  Partner B *Yes, he is. Are you happy?*
  Partner A *Yes, I am.* OR *No, I'm not.*

3

6

9

8

a Look at the words and the pictures.
Write what the people are.

a bus driver   policemen   a nurse
a teacher   doctors   an astronaut ✔
musicians   an artist   a vet
photographers   a fisherman

▶ *He's an astronaut.*

1 ....

2 ....

3 ....

4 ....

5 ....

6 ....

7 ....

8 ....

9 ....

10 ....

b Ask your teacher if you can play a class game.
First, spend a minute saying all the jobs you can
think of. Ask your teacher to write them on
the board for you. Now play the game like this:

▶ Pupil A   *I'm a greengrocer.*
   Pupil B   *I'm a builder.*
   Pupil C   *I'm a dentist.*
   Pupil D   *I'm a secretary.*

Say a new sentence each time. If you can't, you
drop out of the game.

9 Work with a partner. Look at the picture.
How many things can you say about it?

▶ Partner A   *He's small.*
   Partner B   *She's happy.*
   Partner A   *They're green.*
   Partner B   *They're old.*

There's and there are

I'm bored. What can I do?

Come to Wibble!
There's a sweet factory, **there are** restaurants, **there's** a swimming-pool, **there are** slides and swings.

I Tick (✔) the correct boxes.

- Is there a swimming-pool in Wibble?
  Yes ☐   No ☐

- How does Splodge know what's in Wibble?
  Because he lives in Wibble. ☐
  Because he doesn't live in Wibble. ☐

GRAMMAR

A

there's (there is) and **there are** are to talk about things you can see or things that you know exist.

> **There's** a bee on my T-shirt.
> **There's** a school in my town.
> **There are** books on my desk.
> **There are** trees in the park.

2 Write four things that you can see or that you know exist. Use **there's** or **there are**.

▶ There's a school in my town.

There are books on my desk.

....

....

....

....

B

Use **there's** with one thing, and **there are** with two or more.

One	Two or more
There's a school in Wibble.	*There are two schools in Wibble.*
There's a toyshop.	*There are five toyshops.*
There's a playground.	*There are lots of playgrounds.*

3 Look at the words below. Put them in the correct column.

a school ✔   three shops ✔   four restaurants   a bank
a post office   two cinemas

There's …   **There are …**

▶ a school. ....   three shops. ....

....

....

C

Question	Short answer		
Is there?	**Yes, there is.**	OR	**No, there isn't.**
Is there?	**Yes, there is.**	OR	**No, there isn't.**
Are there?	**Yes, there are.**	OR	**No, there aren't.**
Are there?	**Yes, there are.**	OR	**No, there aren't.**

4

a Write four questions. Use the words below to help you.

a castle ✔   toyshops ✔   banks   parks
a school   a sweet factory

▶ Is there a castle? ....

Are there toyshops? ....

....

....

....

b Answer these questions. Use short answers.

▶ Is there a castle in your town?
Yes, there is. .... OR No, there isn't. ....

Are there restaurants in your town?
Yes, there are. .... OR No, there aren't. ....

1 Is there a post office in your town?
....

2 Is there an airport in your town?
....

3 Are there shops in your town?
....

4 Are there chocolate factories in your town?
....

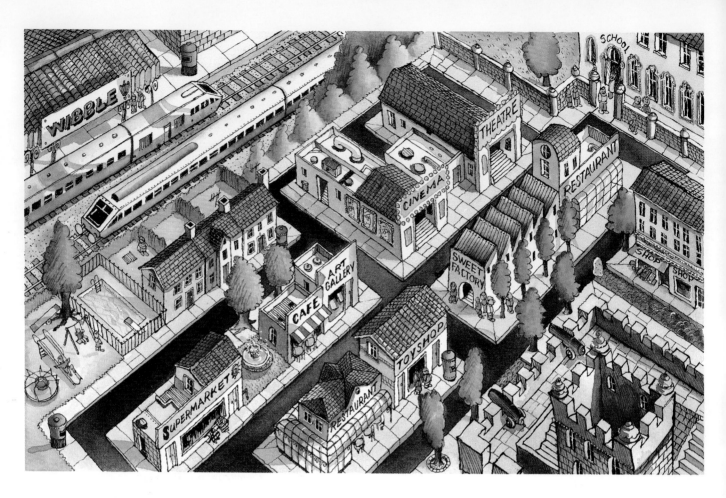

PRACTICE

5

a Look at the map. What is there in Wibble?
Write ten sentences. Use the words below.

an art gallery ✔   postboxes ✔   a café
a supermarket   restaurants   a station
a playground   a castle   houses
shops   trees   swimming-pool

▶ There's an art gallery.

There are four postboxes.

....

....

....

....

....

....

....

....

....

....

b Work with a partner. What else can you see in
Wibble? Take turns to say five sentences each.
Use the words below to help you.

fountain ✔   children ✔   sweet factory
toyshop   station   houses   roads
cinema   café   supermarket
restaurants   theatre

▶ Partner A   *There's a fountain.*
Partner B   *There are children.*

6

a Make the sentences into questions.

▶ There's a station.

   Is there a station?..................................

   There are houses.

   Are there houses?..................................

1 There are banks.

   ....

2 There's a fountain.

   ....

3 There are cafés.

   ....

4 There's an art gallery.

   ....

5 There are restaurants.

   ....

6 There's a supermarket.

   ....

7 There are toyshops.

   ....

8 There's a swimming-pool.

   ....

9 There are schools.

   ....

10 There's a sweet factory.

   ....

b Work with a partner. Make questions about your town. Take turns to ask and answer your questions.

▶ Partner A   *Is there a car park?*
   Partner B   *No, there isn't. Is there a fountain?*
   Partner A   *Yes, there is.*

7

a Work in small groups. Imagine your ideal town. What is there in it? You can have anything you like! Take turns to make suggestions. Write your ideas here:

   ....

   ....

   ....

   ....

   ....

   ....

   ....

   ....

b Now take a large piece of paper. Draw a picture of your town. Write 'shop', 'school', 'trees' etc on your drawing. When you have finished, give your paper to another group. Ask them to describe your town.

▶ Pupil A   *There are lots of flowers.*
   Pupil B   *There's a very big playground.*
   Pupil C   *There's a funfair.*
   Pupil D   *There are two sweet factories.*

8

a Ask your teacher to help you. Tumble, Ruff and Splodge are on a desert island. What do you think there is on the island? Shut your eyes and try to imagine it. Ask your teacher to write your ideas on the board for you.

▶ Pupil A   *On the island there's a river.*
   Pupil B   *On the island there are tall coconut trees.*
   Pupil C   *On the island there are boats.*
   Pupil D   *On the island there's a big jungle.*

b Draw the island and write about it, either on your own for homework, or with a friend.

16 Have got

LOOK AT MY PRESENTS. I'VE GOT A NEW BICYCLE.

I'VE GOT A RACING CAR.

I'VE GOT A COMPUTER GAME.

BUT YOU **HAVEN'T GOT** A COMPUTER !

1 True or false? Tick (✔) the correct boxes.

- Mo has got a racing car.   True ☐   False ☐
- Mo has got a computer.   True ☐   False ☐

GRAMMAR

A

have got is to say that you own something.

> *I've got a new jacket.*
> *He's got a computer game.*
> *We've got bicycles.*

2 Write four things that you own.

▶ I've got a bicycle.

....

....

....

....

B

have got is also to describe people, animals and things.

> *I've got blue eyes.*
> *She's got a nice smile.*
> *We've got short hair.*

3 Write two sentences to describe yourself and two sentences to describe a friend.

▶ I've got blue eyes.   She's got brown hair.

....

....

C

Positive +

I**'ve got**
you**'ve got**
he**'s got**
she**'s got**
it**'s got**
we**'ve got**
you**'ve got**
they**'ve got**

See page 170.

4 Write the correct form of **have got** in the gaps.

▶ My friend Mo *has got* a cat.

I *'ve got* two cats and a hamster.

1 He .... a brown dog.

2 It .... a brown body and black ears.

3 We .... some birds.

4 They .... red and yellow feathers.
They're beautiful.

D

Negative –

I **haven't got**
you **haven't got**
he **hasn't got**
she **hasn't got**
it **hasn't got**
we **haven't got**
you **haven't got**
they **haven't got**

See page 170.

5 Make the positive sentences negative.
Use **haven't got** or **hasn't got**.

▶ Mo has got a rabbit.

Mo hasn't got a rabbit.

1 Snapper has got a new book.

....

2 Mo's friend has got brown eyes.

....

3 Mo's father has got a big car.

....

4 I've got a biscuit.

....

E

Question	Short answer		
Have I **got**?	Yes, I **have**.	OR	No, I **haven't**.
Have you **got**?	Yes, you **have**.	OR	No, you **haven't**.
Has he **got**?	Yes, he **has**.	OR	No, he **hasn't**.
Has she **got**?	Yes, she **has**.	OR	No, she **hasn't**.
Has it **got**?	Yes, it **has**.	OR	No, it **hasn't**.
Have we **got**?	Yes, we **have**.	OR	No, we **haven't**.
Have you **got**?	Yes, you **have**.	OR	No, you **haven't**.
Have they **got**?	Yes, they **have**.	OR	No, they **haven't**.

6

a Read the questions. Tick the correct boxes.

Have you got a brother?	Yes ☐	No ☐
Have you got blue eyes?	Yes ☐	No ☐
Have you got a watch?	Yes ☐	No ☐
Have you got a pet lion?	Yes ☐	No ☐

b Take turns to ask and answer the questions round the class. Use **yes, I have** or **no, I haven't**.

PRACTICE

7 Think of a person you know. Write ten sentences to describe him or her. Use **he's got** or **she's got** and **he hasn't got** or **she hasn't got**.

▶ *She's got brown eyes.*   *She hasn't got long hair.*

1 ....   6 ....

2 ....   7 ....

3 ....   8 ....

4 ....   9 ....

5 ....   10 ....

8

a Snapper is looking at his toys. Write what he's got. Use the words in the list.

paintbrushes   a train   two cars   a puzzle   a book
a telescope   a teddy bear   a football   an aeroplane ✔
marbles   cards

▶ *He's got an aeroplane.*

....

....

....

....

....

b Work with a partner. Look at the picture. Take turns to ask and answer these questions. Use **yes, he has** or **no, he hasn't** for your answers.

Has Snapper got two trains?
Has Snapper got a football?
Has Snapper got five teddy bears?
Has Snapper got marbles?
Has Snapper got a computer?

▶ Partner A   *Has Snapper got an aeroplane?*
   Partner B   *Yes, he has. Has Snapper got two trains?*

9 Mo's friends are making a list of their things. Look at the pictures and write what they have got and haven't got.

We've got

We haven't got

▶ They've got a football. . . . .   They haven't got a boat. . . . .

. . . .

. . . .

. . . .

. . . .

. . . .

10

a Draw an imaginary animal or a monster on a piece of paper. Now write ten sentences about it. Use **has got**.

b Swap drawings with a partner. Describe your partner's animal to the class.

▶ It's got three legs. . . . .

1 . . . .   6 . . . .

2 . . . .   7 . . . .

3 . . . .   8 . . . .

4 . . . .   9 . . . .

5 . . . .   10 . . . .

▶ *It's got green fur. It's got a big mouth and long ears.*

11 Answer the questions. Use short answers.

► Have you got an uncle?   Yes, I have. OR No, I haven't.

1 Has your neighbour got a garden? ....

2 Have you got two noses? ....

3 Has your school got a playground? ....

4 Have your parents got a car? ....

5 Has your best friend got ten fingers? ....

6 Have you got a pet crocodile? ....

7 Has your town got a park? ....

8 Have you got an English book? ....

9 Has your doctor got brown hair? ....

10 Have your friends got pet snakes? ....

12

a Think of a person the whole class knows.
Write five sentences about the person. Use **has got**.

► She's got blue eyes. ....

1 ....

2 ....

3 ....

4 ....

5 ....

b Now read your sentences to the class.
Ask them to guess who you are describing.

► Pupil A   *She's got a red shirt. She's got long brown hair. She's got*
                 a nice face. She's got a cat. She's got two children.
   Class   *Is it the head teacher?*

13 Play a class game. Take turns to say what you've each got.
Listen very carefully. Play the game like this:

► Pupil A   *I've got a football.*
   Pupil B   *I've got a football and a rocket.*
   Pupil C   *I've got a football, a rocket and a computer.*
   Pupil D   *I've got a football, a rocket, a computer and a tiger.*

Imperatives

1 Tick (✔) the correct boxes.

• What does Spike want?   The ball ☐   A sweet ☐

• Is Snapper helping Mo?   Yes ☐   No ☐

GRAMMAR

A

Imperatives are to tell someone to do something or not to do something.

> **Give** *me that ball.*   **Don't touch** *the dog. He bites.*
> **Come** *here.*   **Don't hit** *me.*
> **Eat** *him.*   **Don't stand** *in the road.*

2 Circle the imperatives.

Snapper, (come) here. Help me. I'm hiding from Spike. Come quickly, I need you. Run, Snapper. I'm in the kitchen. Close the window, Spike can see us. Give me the ball. I don't want Spike to have it. Shut the door. Don't laugh, it isn't funny. Sit here. Be quiet and don't make a noise. Good! I think Spike is going now.

B

It's easy to make imperatives. Just use the base verb.

> **Listen** *to me.*   **Look** *at the crocodile.*
> **Watch.**   *Snapper,* **run.**
> **Sit** *down, Mo.*   **Stand** *up.*
> **Come** *here.*   **Go** *away.*

3 Write four imperatives.

▶ Watch................   Jump...........................

....

....

C

There are positive and negative imperatives.

Positive +	Negative –
base verb	**don't** + base verb
Listen.	*Don't listen.*
Look.	*Don't look.*
Run.	*Don't run.*

4 Make the positive imperatives negative.

▶ Listen.   Don't listen. ....

1 Smile.   ....

2 Open the window.   ....

3 Sit down.   ....

4 Look at Snapper.   ....

 PRACTICE

5

a Match the opposites.

▶ Don't laugh.	Don't write your name.
1 Look at the board.	Don't shut the door.
2 Don't talk.	Laugh.
3 Write your name.	Look out of the window.
4 Don't look out of the window.	Talk.
5 Shut the door.	Don't look at the board.

6 Listen to me.	Hit him.
7 Draw a picture.	Don't shout.
8 Don't run.	Run.
9 Don't hit him.	Don't draw a picture.
10 Shout.	Don't listen to me.

b Work with a partner. Take turns to ask and answer questions.
Use the imperatives in **5a**.

▶ Partner A   *What's the opposite of 'Don't laugh'?*
   Partner B   *'Laugh.' What's the opposite of 'Look at the board'?*

6 Turn the positive imperatives into negatives, and the negatives into positives.

▶ Make me a sandwich.

Don't make me a sandwich.

Don't look at him.

Look at him.

1 Open the door.

....

2 Don't answer the telephone.

....

3 Give him a biscuit.

....

4 Don't sing.

....

5 Sit down.

....

6 Don't jump.

....

7 Shout.

....

8 Don't shut the window.

....

9 Stand up.

....

10 Don't go to sleep.

....

7 Look at the picture of Mo's school friends. What do you think the teacher says when she comes in? Use the words in the list.

play the radio   shout ✔   fight   fly paper aeroplanes
throw books   eat   draw on the board   stand on your chair
throw paper on the floor   drink lemonade   go to sleep

▶ Don't shout. ....

....
....
....
....
....
....
....
....
....
....

8 Fill in the gaps. Use an imperative.

Snapper is eating too fast.

Mo says, ► 'Don't eat............... (eat) so fast.'

Mo is climbing a tree. His mother says,

(1) '......................... (be) careful.'

Mo is copying his friend's homework. His teacher is

angry. She says, (2) '......................... (copy)

Jack's homework.'

Snapper's radio is too loud. Mo says, 'Please

(3) .... (turn) it down.'

Mo can't do his Maths homework. He wants

Snapper to help him. Mo says, 'Snapper,

(4) .... (help) me.

(5) .... (do) my homework for me,

please.'

Mo is shouting at his sister. His mother doesn't like

shouting. She says, 'Mo, (6) .... (shout)

at your sister.'

Mo's sister is throwing her toys at Snapper. Snapper is

angry. He says, (7) '......................... (throw)

your toys at me!'

Snapper doesn't want to have a bath. Mo says he's dirty.

Mo says, (8) '......................... (have) a bath now,

Snapper. You're very dirty.'

Mo wants to drive his father's car. He can't drive.

Snapper says, (9) '......................... (drive) the car,

Mo. It's dangerous.'

Snapper has got Mo's new comic. Mo wants to read the

comic. Mo says, (10) '......................... (give) me

the comic, Snapper!'

9 Work with a partner. Take turns to tell each other what to do, and do it. See the list below for some ideas.

stand up ✔
put your hands on your head ✔
put one hand on your ear
open your mouth
shut your eyes
count to ten
draw a picture of a cat
spell 'rabbit'
touch your nose three times
stand on one leg
make a noise like a dog
put a book on your head
laugh
shut one eye

► Partner A   *Stand up.*
              (Partner B, stand up.)
   Partner B   *Put your hands on your head.*
              (Partner A, put your hands on your head.)

10 Ask your teacher if you can play 'Snapper says'. This is how you play:

Teacher   *Snapper says, 'Put your hands on your head.'*
          (Pupils, put your hands on your heads.)
Teacher   *Snapper says, 'Smile.'*
          (Pupils, smile.)
Teacher   *Stand next to the door.*
          (Pupils, don't move! Only move if your teacher says, 'Snapper says …')

Present simple 1

Speech bubbles:

I don't like Verbs. They **catch** birds, and **eat** them for breakfast. Then they **sleep** in Mildred's bed all day.

Present Simple Verbs **make** loud noises at night and **wake** me up.

The Present Simple is horrible. He's dirty! He never **washes** his hands.

1 Tick (✔) the correct boxes.

• What do Verbs do in the morning?
Have a shower ☐
Eat birds for breakfast ☐

• Does the Present Simple wash his hands?
Yes ☐   No ☐

G GRAMMAR

A

The present simple is to talk about things that you do again and again.

*They **catch** birds.*
*They **make** loud noises at night.*
*He never **washes** his hands.*
*I **go** to school.*

2 What do you do every day? Use the words below to help you. Write four sentences.

go to school ✔   get up   have a bath
have lunch   read a book   talk to a friend
play a game   wash your hands   go to bed

►  ....
....
....
....
....

B

The present simple is easy to make.

Positive +	Negative –
base verb	**don't** + base verb
I **walk**	I **don't walk**
you **walk**	you **don't walk**
we **walk**	we **don't walk**
you **walk**	you **don't walk**
they **walk**	they **don't walk**

See page 170.

3 Fill in the gaps. Use the present simple.

▶ I _go_ to school. (go)

I _don't go_ to school. (not go)

1 We .... television. (watch)

2 We .... television. (not watch)

3 They .... their hands. (wash)

4 They .... their hands. (not wash)

C

Add **s** or **es** with **he**, **she** and **it**.

Positive +	Negative –
base verb + **s/es**	**doesn't** + base verb
he **walks/goes**	he **doesn't walk**
she **walks/goes**	she **doesn't walk**
it **walks/goes**	it **doesn't walk**

See page 170.

4 Fill in the gaps. Use the present simple.

Splodge ▶ _likes_............ (like) books
and comics. He (1) .... (read)
Mo and Snapper comics every day.
On Mondays, he (2) .... (go) to
the shop and he (3) .... (buy)
a new Mo and Snapper comic. Sometimes he
(4) .... (give) the comics to
Tumble. Tumble likes comics, too.

D

Question	Short answer		
Do I **walk**?	Yes, I **do**.	OR	No, I **don't**.
Do you **walk**?	Yes, you **do**.	OR	No, you **don't**.
Does he **walk**?	Yes, he **does**.	OR	No, he **doesn't**.
Does she **walk**?	Yes, she **does**.	OR	No, she **doesn't**.
Does it **walk**?	Yes, it **does**.	OR	No, it **doesn't**.
Do we **walk**?	Yes, we **do**.	OR	No, we **don't**.
Do you **walk**?	Yes, you **do**.	OR	No, you **don't**.
Do they **walk**?	Yes, they **do**.	OR	No, they **don't**.

5 Fill in the gaps to make questions and short answers.

▶ _Do_.....you _read_.........comics? (read)   Yes, _I do._...............

1 ....he ....biscuits? (eat)   No, ...

2 ....we ....English? (learn)   Yes, ...

3 ....she ....to school? (walk)   No, ...

4 ....they ....television? (watch) Yes, ...

E

Learn these!

have breakfast   **have lunch**   **have supper**
have a shower   **have a bath**

I/you/we/you/they have a bath.
he/she/it has a bath.

*They never **have** a shower.*
*Splodge sometimes **has** a shower.*

6 Write four sentences. Use **have** with the words on the left.

► She *has supper at six.*

1 We ....

2 I ....

3 He ....

4 They ....

 PRACTICE

7

a Splodge is talking to some Verbs. Fill in the gaps. Use the present simple.

Verb 1   Why don't you like me, Splodge?

Splodge   Because you ► *eat* .... (eat) birds for breakfast!

Verb 1   No, I don't! I (1) .... (eat) eggs and snails. You (2) .... (cook) mud pies. That's horrible.

Splodge   All Verbs (3) .... (have) birds for breakfast. Everyone knows that. And you're all dirty.

Verb 2   It's not true, Splodge. We (4) .... (not eat) birds. And we're clean. We (5) .... (have) a shower every year.

Splodge   One shower every year! That's really horrible. I (6) .... (wash) my hands every day and I (7) .... (brush) my teeth every night.

Ruff (8) .... (brush) his teeth three times a day!

Verb 1   He's very, very clean! Does Tumble wash every day?

Splodge   Yes, he does. He (9) .... (have) a shower at night.

Verb 2   What does Tumble do in the day?

Splodge   He (10) .... (sleep) in his favourite chair. He's the same as you! Always asleep!

b Work with a partner. Take turns to ask and answer the questions.

► Why doesn't Splodge like Verbs?
1 Do you think Verbs eat birds for breakfast?
2 What does Verb 1 eat for breakfast?
3 What does Splodge cook?
4 How often do Verbs have a shower?
5 Does Splodge wash his hands?
6 Who brushes his teeth three times a day?
7 Who has a shower at night?
8 Who sleeps in a chair?

► Partner A   *Why doesn't Splodge like Verbs?*
   Partner B   *He doesn't like Verbs because they eat birds.*

8

a Write sentences about yourself. Look at the questions below and answer them. Use the present simple.

▶ How often do you wash your hands?
1 When do you get up?
2 Do you have a shower or a bath?
3 When do you have a shower or a bath?
4 What do you eat for breakfast?
5 How do you go to school?
6 Do you watch television?
7 What sport do you play?
8 When do you have supper?
9 Do you cook?
10 When do you sleep?

▶ I wash my hands four times a day.
1 ....
2 ....
3 ....
4 ....
5 ....
6 ....
7 ....
8 ....
9 ....
10 ....

b Swap books with a partner. Now take turns to read the answers to the class. Don't forget **s** or **es** with **he** and **she**!

▶ Pupil A   *Maria washes her hands three times a day.*
   Pupil B   *Peter gets up at half past seven.*

9

a What do you think a Verb does every day? Write a short story. Use the verbs below if you need help. Don't forget **s** or **es**!

get up   go shopping   eat   watch   cook
read   run   swim   have lunch   brush
clean   have a bath   play   talk   make
dance   sing   wash   drink   work
have breakfast   write   sleep

▶ *Every day the Verb wakes up at midnight. He dances with his friends. He makes a lot of noise. At three o'clock in the morning he catches spiders. He eats spiders for breakfast. He drinks hot milk. He brushes his ears and he sings a song.*

THE VERB'S DAY
....
....
....
....
....
....
....
....
....
....

b Now work with a partner. Take turns to ask and answer questions about your Verb stories. Use short answers.

▶ Partner A   *Does your Verb go shopping?*
   Partner B   *Yes, he does.*

   Partner B   *Does your Verb cook?*
   Partner A   *No, he doesn't.*

Present simple 2

1   Tick (✔) the correct boxes.

• Does Mo like Maths?
    Yes ☐   No ☐

• Does Snapper like doing Mo's homework?
    Yes ☐   No ☐

 GRAMMAR

A

Use the present simple with **like**, **love** and **hate**, NOT the present continuous.

| *I **like** sweets.* | NOT | ~~I'm liking sweets.~~ |
| *Mo **hates** Spike.* | NOT | ~~Mo is hating Spike.~~ |

2   Write two things that you like and two things that you hate.

▶

....

....

B

like, **love**, **hate** + noun.

		Noun
I	*like*	*chocolate.*
He	*loves*	*football.*
We	*hate*	*homework.*

3   Write four things you like. Use **like** + noun.

▶   I like weekends.

....

....

....

....

C

like, love, hate + ing form.

	Verb	**ing** form
I	**like**	*reading.*
Mo	**loves**	*playing* football.
Snapper	**hates**	*doing* Mo's homework.

4 Write what Mo loves doing. Use these words.

play football ✔   talk to Snapper

watch television   swim   read comics

▶ Mo loves playing football. ....

....

....

....

....

 PRACTICE

5 Look at the lists. Write sentences.

Snapper likes ...		**Snapper doesn't like ...**	
comics ✔	bananas	Mo's school books ✔	grapes
rabbits	Mo	cats	Mo's neighbour
sunshine	weekends	rain	schooldays

▶ Snapper likes comics .... but he doesn't like Mo's school books. ....

1 Snapper .... but he ....

2 Snapper .... but he ....

3 Snapper .... but he ....

4 Snapper .... but he ....

5 Snapper .... but he ....

6

a Mo is talking to his friend Pad on the telephone. Fill in the gaps. Use the **ing** form.

Mo Snapper and I ▶ love riding .... (love/ride) our bicycles.

We (1) .... (like/swim) but we (2) .... (not like/go) to

school. What sports do you (3) .... (like/do)?

Pad I (4) .... (love/play) tennis with my friends.

We (5) .... (like/fish) in the river. We usually go to the river after school.

Mo I (6) .... (hate/go) to school!

Do you (7) .... (like/go) to school?

Pad Yes, I like going to school. It's fun. I (8) .... (love/see) my friends

and I (9) .... (like/learn) new things. Geography is my favourite lesson.

Mo Snapper (10) .... (love/do) my homework. He likes Maths especially.

Snapper No, I don't! I hate doing Maths.

b Work with a partner. Take turns to ask and answer questions. Use the words below.

play tennis ✔   play football   read
ride a bicycle   cook ✔   go to school
talk to your friends   learn English
do homework   swim   watch television

▶ Partner A   *Do you like playing tennis?*
Partner B   *Yes, I like playing tennis.*

Partner B   *Do you like cooking?*
Partner A   *No, I don't like cooking.*

7

a Read the sentences. Are they true or false? If they're false, write the correct answer.

▶ Cats love dogs.
  False. Cats don't like dogs.

  Dogs love chasing cats.
  True.

1 Rabbits like meat.
  ....

2 Cats hate chasing mice.
  ....

3 Mice like cheese.
  ....

4 Fish don't like water.
  ....

5 Birds love eating worms.
  ....

6 Cows don't like grass.
  ....

7 Birds hate flying.
  ....

8 Dogs don't like going for walks.
  ....

9 Rabbits hate eating carrots.
  ....

10 Cats like milk.
  ....

b Work with a partner. Take turns to ask and answer questions.

▶ Partner A   *Do cats love dogs?*
Partner B   *No, they don't. They hate dogs.*

Partner B   *Do dogs love chasing cats?*
Partner A   *Yes, they do.*

8

a Write five things that you love and five things that you hate. Use a noun or an **ing** form.

► I love omelettes.   I hate Maths.

I love writing letters.   I hate cooking.

....

....

....

....

....

b Swap books with a partner. Take turns to tell the class what your partner loves and hates.

► *She loves bananas.*
She hates getting up early.

9 Work with a partner. Invent two characters: a boy and a girl. Give them names. Write a list of three things that they love and three things that they hate.

► Dr Mad-Hat loves making cakes.

Mrs Hardhead hates spiders.

....

....

....

....

....

....

....

....

....

....

10 Work in small groups. Look at the list below. Find two things you all like, two things you all love and two things you all hate. Tell the class.

going to bed   chicken
English   puzzles
doing homework   games
reading books   washing up
lemonade   getting presents
playing   shopping
peanuts   lemons
tidying your bedroom   chocolate biscuits
cooking   Maths
getting up early   salad
school   films
having a birthday   going to the doctor's
coffee   break time
going on holiday   school holidays
watching cartoons

► *We like English and Geography.*
We love chocolate biscuits and ice cream.
We hate tidying our bedrooms and washing up.

WE LOVE CYCLING. SNAPPER DOES ALL THE WORK.

Present continuous

1 Tick (✔) the correct boxes.

- What's Splodge doing in the picture?
  He's eating. ☐   He's singing. ☐
  He's standing on his head. ☐

- Who's teaching Splodge?
  Tumble ☐   Mildred's parrot ☐   Ruff ☐

GRAMMAR

A

The present continuous is to talk about things
that are happening *now*.

> *I'm learning* new words.
> *He's teaching* me.
> Splodge *is standing* on his head.

2 Circle the verbs that are in the present
continuous.

Splodge (is learning) new words. 'Hippopotamus'
is a new word. Mildred's parrot is teaching him.
Tumble and Ruff are watching Splodge.
They're talking to him. They want to know
why he's standing on his head. Splodge wants
the words to stay in his head. Do you stand on
your head when you're learning new words?

B

It's easy to make the present continuous
of most verbs:

be + base verb + **ing**

Positive +	Negative –
I'm eating	**I'm not eating**
you**'re eating**	you **aren't eating**
he**'s eating**	he **isn't eating**
she**'s eating**	she **isn't eating**
it**'s eating**	it **isn't eating**
we**'re eating**	we **aren't eating**
you**'re eating**	you **aren't eating**
they**'re eating**	they **arcn't eating**

See page 170.

3 Complete the sentences.

▶ We ....re drinking........... (drink) milk.

1 I .... (read) a book.

2 He .... (eat) a mud pie.

3 They .... (watch) Splodge.

4 She .... (teach) English.

C

Question	Short answer		
Am I working?	Yes, I **am**.	OR	No, **I'm not**.
Are you **working?**	Yes, you **are**.	OR	No, you **aren't**.
Is he **working?**	Yes, he **is**.	OR	No, he **isn't**.
Is she **working?**	Yes, she **is**.	OR	No, she **isn't**.
Is it **working?**	Yes, it **is**.	OR	No, it **isn't**.
Are we **working?**	Yes, we **are**.	OR	No, we **aren't**.
Are you **working?**	Yes, you **are**.	OR	No, you **aren't**.
Are they **working?**	Yes, they **are**.	OR	No, they **aren't**.

4 Make four questions. Use the present continuous.

▶ ..Is..... Splodge ..reading........... (read) his dictionary?

1 .... Mabel .... (drink) coffee?

2 .... Ruff and Tumble .... (watch) television?

3 .... you .... (read) a book?

4 .... I .... (learn) English?

D

Be careful! Some verbs end in **e**.
Take away **e** and add **ing**.

*The sun **is shining**.*	NOT	~~shineing~~
*Mabel **is coming**.*	NOT	~~comeing~~
*Splodge **is smiling**.*	NOT	~~smileing~~
*Ruff **is writing**.*	NOT	~~writeing~~

5 Fill in the gaps.

▶ The sun ..is shining............... (shine).

1 She .... (bake) a cake.

2 He .... (drive) a car.

3 I .... (make) a milkshake.

4 You .... (write) a letter.

REMEMBER!

These are vowels: **a, e, i, o, u**

These are consonants:
b, c, d, f, g, h, j, k, l, m, n, p, q, r, s, t, v, w, x, y, z

See Chapter 38.

6 How many vowels are there in this sentence? How many consonants are there?

Splodge is drinking Fizzy Ink.

There are .... vowels.

There are .... consonants.

E

Some verbs end in a vowel + consonant.
Be careful! Always double the consonant.

swim	→ *swimming*	stop	→ *stopping*
run	→ *running*	get	→ *getting*
sit	→ *sitting*	put	→ *putting*

*Splodge **is running** to the sweet shop.*
*Tumble **is sitting** down.*
*Ruff **is putting** his coat on.*

7 Fill in the gaps. Use the present continuous.

► She's in her car. She's stopping (stop) the car.

1 He .... (put) his T-shirt on.

2 She .... (run) upstairs.

3 I .... (sit) in a chair.

4 Mabel is at the seaside.

   She .... (swim) in the sea.

8

a Write sentences in the present continuous. Use the words below.

► drink / Fizzy Ink		6 watch / television
1 drive / a car		7 carry / the shopping
2 eat / a sandwich		8 write / a letter
3 bake / a cake		9 run / to school
4 tidy / the kitchen		10 listen / to music
5 ride / a bicycle		

► Splodge is drinking Fizzy Ink ....

1 Mildred ....

2 Tumble ....

3 Mabel ....

4 Mabel and Ruff ....

5 I ....

6 Splodge ....

7 Splodge and Tumble ....

   ....

8 You ....

9 The boy ....

10 We ....

b Work with a partner. Take turns to ask and answer these questions.

► Who's drinking Fizzy Ink?

1 Who's driving a car?

2 Who's eating a sandwich?

3 Who's baking a cake?

4 Who's tidying the kitchen?

5 Who's watching television?

6 Who's carrying the shopping?

► Partner A   *Who's drinking Fizzy Ink?*
  Partner B   *Splodge is drinking Fizzy Ink.*

9 Look at the questions. Answer them using a short answer.

▶ Are you writing a letter now?
Yes, I am. OR No, I'm not. ....

1 Are you reading a book?
....

2 Is your teacher standing on his or her head?
....

3 Are your friends listening to the teacher?
....

4 Are you sitting at your desk?
....

5 Is your teacher writing on the board?
....

6 Is the sun shining?
....

7 Is it raining now?
....

8 Are you learning Maths now?
....

9 Are your friends speaking English?
....

10 Are you singing a song?
....

10 Write what everybody is doing in Splodge's house now. Use the present continuous.

▶ Sticky / drink / carrot juice.
Sticky is drinking carrot juice.

1 Splodge / eat / mud pies
....

2 Tumble / not read / a newspaper
....

3 Ruff / cut / Splodge's hair
....

4 Mabel and Mildred / not listen / to Splodge
....

5 Mabel's cat / climb / a tree
....

6 Mildred / bake / a cake
....

7 Ruff's machine / make / spaghetti
....

8 Mildred's parrot / fly
....

9 Tumble / not / drink / coffee
....

10 Splodge / play / the violin
....

11 Play a miming game. Take turns to mime an action. The class tries to guess what you're doing. Here are some ideas:

riding a bicycle	riding an elephant
driving a very fast car	frying an egg
walking on hot sand	eating an ice cream
climbing a mountain	writing a letter
taking a dog for a walk	eating spaghetti
conducting an orchestra	feeding a lion
carrying a very heavy bag	drinking Fizzy Ink
swimming in cold water	carrying a feather

▶ Class   *Are you climbing a mountain?*
  Pupil   *Yes, I am.* OR *No, I'm not.*

 **Present simple and continuous**

TODAY IS A HOLIDAY. WHY **ARE** WE **GOING** FOR A WALK? WE USUALLY **WATCH** TELEVISION ALL DAY.

IT'S SPRING! THE SUN **IS** SHINING. THE BIRDS **ARE SINGING**. IT'S BEAUTIFUL. IT**'S**...

...RAINING!

SO WHAT'S ON TELEVISION TODAY?

I Tick (✔) the correct boxes.

• What do Snapper and Mo usually do all day?
Read books ☐   Watch television ☐

• Look at pictures 1 and 2.
What are Mo and Snapper doing now?
Watching television ☐   Going for a walk ☐

 GRAMMAR

REMEMBER!

The present simple is to talk about things that you do again and again.

> *We usually **watch** television all day.*
> *I **go** to school.*
> *She **reads** a book every night.*

See Chapter 18.

2 Circle the verbs in the present simple. How many are there?

Mo (goes) to school every weekday. Snapper reads comics and watches television. Mo usually plays football with his friends in the afternoon. Snapper and Mo have supper at seven o'clock. Then they watch television.

There are .... verbs in the present simple.

REMEMBER!

The present continuous is to talk about things that are happening *now*.

> *They**'re going** for a walk.*
> *The birds **are singing**.*
> *Mo **is talking**.*

See Chapter 20.

3 Circle the verbs in the present continuous. How many are there?

Mo and Snapper (are going) for a walk. It's a nice day. The sun is shining and the birds are singing. Mo and Snapper are walking in the park. Mo is singing a song and Snapper is laughing.

There are .... verbs in the present continuous.

A

Present simple = again and again.

Present continuous = now.

Look at the differences.

> *I **get up** at seven o'clock.*
> = Every day I get up at seven o'clock.
> *I'm **getting up**.*
> = I'm getting up now.
>
> *They **play** football after school.*
> = They always play football after school.
> *They're **playing** football.*
> = They're playing football now.

4 Look at the sentences below.
Put them in the correct columns.

Snapper reads comics every day. ✔
Snapper is reading a comic. ✔
Mo is walking to school.
Snapper watches television in the afternoon.
Snapper is watching television.
Mo walks to school at eight o'clock.

Present simple

▶ Snapper reads comics every day.

1 ....

....

2 ....

....

Present continuous

Snapper is reading a comic.

3 ....

....

4 ....

....

5 Fill in the gaps. Use the present simple or present continuous of the words in brackets. Think carefully!

▶ Mo usually gets up (get up) at half past seven but today he 's getting up (get up) late because it's a holiday.

1 He usually .... (have) a shower but today he .... (have) a bath.

2 Mo and Snapper usually .... (stay) at home and watch television when they're on holiday but today they .... (go) for a walk.

3 Mo usually .... (make) the sandwiches for their walks but today Snapper .... (make) them.

4 They usually .... (have) peanut butter sandwiches but today they .... (have) fish sandwiches.

5 They usually .... (take) their dog on their walks but today they .... (leave) the dog at home.

6 Mo is having a bad dream. Everything is wrong! Look at the two lists below. Fill in the gaps in the sentences. Use the present simple and the present continuous.

Usually	**Today**
▶ have a shower	have a cold bath
1 drink orange juice	drink black coffee
2 eat toast and jam	eat carrots and lettuce
3 read a comic	read a newspaper
4 watch television	listen to the radio
5 wear a T-shirt	wear a shirt and tie

▶ Mo usually *has a shower* ....
but today he *'s having a cold bath.*

1 He usually ....
but today he...

2 He usually ....
but today he...

3 He usually ....
but today he...

4 He usually ....
but today he...

5 He usually ....
but today he ....

7 Work with a partner. Imagine that Snapper is having a bad day. He isn't doing anything nice. Write sentences about the nice things he usually does and the nasty things he's doing today.

▶ *Snapper usually goes to the cinema but* ....
today he's cleaning the kitchen.
He usually eats chocolate but today he's
eating peas.
....
....
....
....
....
....
....
....
....
....
....
....
....
....
....

Past simple 1

Splodge, wake up!

I drank Ruff's magic potion. In my dream I **was** very handsome and then I **was** a pop star and I **was** very famous and then I **was** a doctor and I **was** clever and then ... you said 'Wake up!'

MAGIC DREAMS Potion

---

1 Tick (✔) the correct boxes.

- Is Splodge a doctor now?
  Yes ☐   No ☐

- Was Splodge a doctor in his dream?
  Yes ☐   No ☐

 GRAMMAR

REMEMBER!

The present simple of **be** is to talk about yourself, other people, animals or things *now*.

> *I'm happy.*
> *She's a doctor.*
> *We're at school.*

See Chapter 14.

2 Write four things about yourself or a friend.

▶ I'm a boy. ....

Sophie is my friend. ....

....

....

....

....

A

The past simple of **be** is to talk about yourself, other people, animals or things *before now*. Look:

today	yesterday, last week, last year etc
I'm a doctor.	*I **was** a doctor.*
He's at school.	*He **was** at school.*
We're hungry.	*We **were** hungry.*

3 Rewrite the sentences.
Use the past simple of **be**.

▶ I'm happy.

I <u>was</u> happy.

1 He's angry.

He .... angry.

2 I'm a teacher.

I .... a teacher.

3 We're schoolchildren.

We .... schoolchildren.

4 Splodge's rabbit is hungry.

Splodge's rabbit .... hungry.

B

Make the past simple of **be** like this:

Positive +
I **was**
you **were**
he **was**
she **was**
it **was**
we **were**
you **were**
they **were**

4 Write four sentences. Use the words below.

astronauts ✔   a doctor   happy   funny
film stars

▶ They <u>were astronauts.</u>

1 She ....

2 They ....

3 He ....

4 We ....

C

Negative –
I **wasn't**
you **weren't**
he **wasn't**
she **wasn't**
it **wasn't**
we **weren't**
you **weren't**
they **weren't**

See back cover.

5 Fill in the gaps. Use the negative.

Ruff Mabel was angry with you yesterday, Splodge.

Splodge No, she ▶ <u>wasn't</u>! I (1) ....
naughty. I was good and I was very polite.

Ruff Mabel says you (2) .... good. She says
you put big worms in her bed.

Splodge But Mabel likes worms! She (3) ....
angry. The worms (4) .... big, they were
small and pink. They were very nice worms.

22 Past simple I   **89**

D

Question	Short answer		
Was I?	Yes, I **was**.	OR	No, I **wasn't**.
Were you?	Yes, you **were**.	OR	No, you **weren't**.
Was he?	Yes, he **was**.	OR	No, he **wasn't**.
Was she?	Yes, she **was**.	OR	No, she **wasn't**.
Was it?	Yes, it **was**.	OR	No, it **wasn't**.
Were we?	Yes, we **were**.	OR	No, we **weren't**.
Were you?	Yes, you **were**.	OR	No, you **weren't**.
Were they?	Yes, they **were**.	OR	No, they **weren't**.

6 Fill in the gaps to make questions and answers.

▶ ...*Was*..... Splodge's dream a nice dream? Yes, *it was*.....

1 .... Mabel angry with Splodge? Yes, ...

2 .... Splodge very small in his dream? No, ...

3 .... Splodge a film star in his dream? No, ...

4 .... you happy yesterday? Yes, ...

 PRACTICE

7 Ruff's potion makes lots of dreams.
Look at the pictures. What happened?
Use **was** and the words below.

a chef   a secretary   a king ✔   a clown
a dancer   a singer   a poet   a teacher
a nurse   a footballer   a train driver

In Splodge's dream …

1 Splodge ▶ *was a king* .... and
Mabel ....

2 Mildred .... and
Splodge ....

3 Tumble .... and
Splodge ....

4 Mildred .... ,
Ruff .... and
Tumble ....

5 Ruff .... and
Mabel ....

1

3

5

8 Work with a partner. Look at the picture in **7** again. Take turns to ask and answer the questions about Splodge's dream.

▶ Was Mildred a secretary?
1 Was Mabel a singer?
2 Was Splodge a teacher?
3 Was Mildred a footballer?
4 Was Splodge a train driver?
5 Was Tumble a dancer?
6 Was Ruff a nurse?
7 Was Splodge a poet?
8 Was Tumble a clown?

▶ Partner A *Was Mildred a secretary?*
  Partner B *No, she wasn't.*
       Was Mabel a singer?

2

4

9

a Imagine you and the friends in your class were alive five hundred years ago. What do you think you were? Write ten sentences. Use the list of jobs below if you want help.

a dentist	a nurse	an actor
a teacher	a scientist	a singer
a dancer	a doctor	a writer
a farmer	a fisherman	a pirate
a soldier	a judge	a sailor

▶ I think that Richard was a pirate.

1 ....
2 ....
3 ....
4 ....
5 ....
6 ....
7 ....
8 ....
9 ....
10 ....

b Now take turns to read your sentences to the class, like this:

▶ Pupil A *Richard, I think you were a pirate.*

10 Ask your teacher if you can play a class game. Imagine you drank Ruff's magic dream potion last night. In your dream there was a very strange animal. Describe the animal. Use **was** and **were**.

▶ Pupil A *It was a big animal.*
  Pupil B *Its eyes were green.*
  Pupil C *It was furry.*
  Pupil D *It was frightening.*

Past simple 2

I Tick (✔) the correct boxes.

• Is the biscuit jar smashed now?
Yes ☐   No ☐

• Who do you think smashed the biscuit jar?
Mo ☐   Snapper ☐

GRAMMAR

A

The past simple is to talk about things that are finished. It's for a time *before now*.

> Mo **smashed** the biscuit jar.
> We **played** football in the park last week.
> He **didn't want** a biscuit.
> I **didn't watch** television yesterday.

2 Circle the verbs. They are in the past simple.

Mo (wanted) some biscuits. First, he opened the kitchen door very quietly. Then he walked into the kitchen and opened the cupboard. He picked up the biscuit jar but then he dropped it!

B

Add **ed** or **d** to most verbs.

want	→ *wanted*	play	→ *played*
dance	→ *danced*	smile	→ *smiled*

It's the same for everybody.

Positive +

I help**ed**	I smile**d**
you help**ed**	you smile**d**
he help**ed**	he smile**d**
she help**ed**	she smile**d**
it help**ed**	it smile**d**
we help**ed**	we smile**d**
you help**ed**	you smile**d**
they help**ed**	they smile**d**

3 Make these verbs past simple. Add **ed** or **d**.

► laugh   smile
  laughed   smiled

1 cook   3 like

....

2 wash   4 arrive

....

REMEMBER!

These are consonants.

b, c, d, f, g, h, j, k, l, m, n, p, q, r, s, t, v, w, x, y, z

See Chapter 38.

4 How many consonants are there in this word?
Tick the correct box.

alphabet

Seven ☐   Five ☐   Ten ☐

C

Some verbs end in a consonant + **y**.
Change **y** to **i** and add **ed**.

cr**y** → cr**ied**   tr**y** → tr**ied**
tid**y** → tid**ied**   stud**y** → stud**ied**

I tidied my room yesterday.
She tried to open the window.
We studied English and French last year.

5 Write the verb in the past simple.

▶ I *tidied*.......... (tidy) my room.

1 Mo's sister .... (cry) yesterday.

2 Snapper .... (carry) Mo's books
upstairs after school.

3 Mo .... (study) French last year.

4 They .... (try) to do some
homework in the evening.

D

Be careful! Learn these verbs.

stop → *stopped*   drop → *dropped*
Mo dropped the biscuit jar.
He stopped playing football at four o'clock.

6 Fill in the gaps.

1 Mo .... (drop) his books.

2 Mo and Snapper .... (stop) laughing.

E

To make the negative of the past simple,
use **didn't** + base verb.

Negative –
I **didn't finish**
you **didn't finish**
he **didn't finish**
she **didn't finish**
it **didn't finish**
we **didn't finish**
you **didn't finish**
they **didn't finish**

See back cover.

7 Make the verbs negative.

▶ Snapper dropped the biscuit jar.
Snapper didn't drop the biscuit jar...........

1 Mo studied French last year.
....

2 Mo's sister played with her toys yesterday.
....

3 Snapper helped Mo with his homework.
....

4 Mo wanted to watch television.
....

F

Question	Short answer		
Did I **finish?**	Yes, I **did.**	OR	No, I **didn't.**
Did you **finish?**	Yes, you **did.**	OR	No, you **didn't.**
Did he **finish?**	Yes, he **did.**	OR	No, he **didn't.**
Did she **finish?**	Yes, she **did.**	OR	No, she **didn't.**
Did it **finish?**	Yes, it **did.**	OR	No, it **didn't.**
Did we **finish?**	Yes, we **did.**	OR	No, we **didn't.**
Did you **finish?**	Yes, you **did.**	OR	No, you **didn't.**
Did they **finish?**	Yes, they **did.**	OR	No, they **didn't.**

8 Read the questions and answer them.
Use a short answer.

▶ Did you cook lunch yesterday?

  Yes, I did. OR No, I didn't.

1 Did you watch television last night?

  ....

2 Did you paint a picture last weekend?

  ....

3 Did you talk to a friend yesterday?

  ....

4 Did you walk to school this morning?

  ....

SUGAR

HONEY

STRAWBERRY BUBBLE GUM

PRACTICE

9

a Fill in the gaps. Use the past simple.

Last week Mo and Snapper had an idea.

They ► ...*decided*........ to cook for Mo's mum and dad.

Unfortunately, Mo and Snapper can't cook! First, they

(1) .... (walk) to the supermarket.

Mo (2) .... (ask) for some onions and potatoes.

Snapper (3) .... (want) some sugar and honey, too.

Then they (4) .... (look) for a sweet shop. They

bought some strawberry bubble gum and five green lollipops.

When they (5) .... (arrive) home they went into the

kitchen. Mo (6) .... (mix) the onions and potatoes

together and Snapper (7) .... (add) the bubble gum

and the lollipops. Mo (8) .... (bake) the mixture for

three hours. When his mum came into the kitchen she

(9) .... (scream)! Mo looked at Snapper.

'What's wrong?' he asked. Snapper (10) .... (laugh).

'You put the food in the washing-machine, not the oven!'

b Work with a partner. Take turns to ask and answer these
questions.

► What did Mo and Snapper decide to do?
1 What did Mo ask for in the supermarket?
2 What did Snapper want?
3 What shop did they look for next?
4 Where did Snapper and Mo go when they arrived home?
5 Who mixed the onions and potatoes together?
6 Who added the bubble gum and the lollipops?
7 Who screamed?
8 Where did Mo put the mixture?

► Partner A   *What did Mo and Snapper decide to do?*
   Partner B   *They decided to cook.*

10 Look at the things Mo, Snapper and Milly did yesterday. Write sentences. Use the past simple.

▶ Mo / visit / a friend

Mo visited a friend.

1 Milly / watch / television

....

2 Mo / telephone / the vet

....

3 Snapper / listen / to music

....

4 Mo / tidy / the toy cupboard

....

5 Mo's dad / clean / the windows

....

6 Snapper / drop / a glass

....

7 Mo / play / basketball

....

8 Snapper paint / a picture

....

9 Mo / study / for a Biology test

....

10 Milly / help / Mo

....

11

a Make the sentences negative.

▶ Mo cleaned his bicycle.

Mo didn't clean his bicycle.

1 Snapper climbed a tree.

....

....

2 Milly painted a picture.

....

....

3 Mo cooked spaghetti.

....

....

4 Mo washed his dad's car.

....

....

5 Snapper helped Mo.

....

....

6 Milly watched a cartoon on television.

....

....

7 Snapper talked to Mo's teacher.

....

....

8 Mo wanted to make a strawberry milkshake.

....

....

9 Snapper and Mo walked to the park.

....

....

10 They played football with their friends.

....

....

b Say five sentences about what you did or didn't do yesterday. Use the words below.

tidy / bedroom ✔   bake / a cake
play / the piano   brush / teeth
walk / to school   paint / a picture
talk / to a friend   play / a game
wash / hands   help / a friend

▶ *I tidied my bedroom yesterday.* OR
  I didn't tidy my bedroom yesterday.

12

a Write ten questions in the past simple. Use **did you** and the words below.

▶ laugh / yesterday
1 play / football / yesterday afternoon
2 watch / television / last night
3 listen / to music / yesterday
4 wash / your face / this morning
5 telephone / a friend / yesterday
6 talk / to your teacher / yesterday
7 play / with a friend / last weekend
8 paint / a picture / last week
9 help / your mother or father / last week
10 clean / your shoes / this morning

▶ Did you laugh yesterday? ....

1 ....

2 ....

3 ....

4 ....

5 ....

6 ....

7 ....

8 ....

9 ....

10 ....

b Work with a partner. Ask each other the questions. Answer them using a short answer.

▶ Partner A   *Did you laugh yesterday?*
  Partner B   *Yes, I did.* OR *No, I didn't.*
             Did you play football yesterday afternoon?

13 Ask your teacher if you can play a class game. Work in two teams. Your teacher says the verbs below. Make the verbs past simple. Score one point for every correct answer.

ask ✔   try   dance   want   wash ✔
smash   bake   cook   play   look   fry
carry   watch   happen   work   walk
decide   listen   study   pass   laugh
telephone   smile   paint   talk   scream
brush   help   clean   shout

▶ Teacher   *ask*
  Team A   *asked* (Correct. One point.)

  Teacher   *wash*
  Team B   *washed* (Correct. One point.)

Past simple 3

1 Tick (✔) the correct boxes.

*   Is Splodge making mistakes?
    Yes ☐   No ☐

*   Which sentence is correct?
    I met Lionel. ☐   I meeted Lionel. ☐

 GRAMMAR

REMEMBER!

The past simple is to talk about things that are finished. It's for a time *before now*.

> *Splodge **walked** to school yesterday.*
> *He **listened** to his teacher.*
> *Splodge **talked** to his friends.*
> *He **played** lots of games.*

See Chapter 23.

2 Circle the verbs that are in the past simple.

Splodge (walked) to school yesterday. He talked to his friends. They laughed at his jokes. Splodge was very happy. After school, Splodge helped Ruff and then he watched a cartoon on television.

A

Be careful! Some verbs in the past simple don't behave nicely. Look:

Base verb		Past simple (Positive +)		
eat	→	**ate**	NOT	~~eated~~
drink	→	**drank**	NOT	~~drinked~~
go	→	**went**	NOT	~~goed~~
make	→	**made**	NOT	~~maked~~

*They **ate** an ice cream.*
*He **drank** a lot of Fizzy Ink.*
*They **went** to the zoo.*
*Splodge **made** a banana milkshake.*

B

These verbs are *very* important. Learn the past simple forms. It's a good idea to learn them *now* because you won't need to learn them again!

Base verb		Past simple
be	→	**was/were**
buy	→	**bought**
come	→	**came**
do	→	**did**
drink	→	**drank**
drive	→	**drove**
eat	→	**ate**
find	→	**found**
get	→	**got**
give	→	**gave**
go	→	**went**
have	→	**had**
hear	→	**heard**
make	→	**made**
meet	→	**met**
run	→	**ran**
read	→	**read**
say	→	**said**
see	→	**saw**
sing	→	**sang**
sleep	→	**slept**
stand	→	**stood**
swim	→	**swam**
take	→	**took**
think	→	**thought**
write	→	**wrote**

3 Choose the correct verb. Complete the sentences. Use the past simple.

meet ✔   make   go   eat   drink

► They met.............. Lionel.

1 Ruff and Splodge .... to the zoo.

2 Tumble .... some coffee.

3 Ruff .... three apples.

4 Splodge .... a cake.

4 Put the words into the past simple.

Yesterday, Splodge ► heard......... (hear) a new song on the radio. He liked it so he (1) .... (sing) it all day!

Ruff (2) .... (say) it was a terrible song. He asked Splodge to stop singing it. Unfortunately, Splodge (3) .... (find) Tumble's old guitar. He played the guitar and sang the song all night. Ruff (4) .... (sleep) very badly last night!

C

To make the negative,
use **didn't** + base verb.

Negative –

I **didn't sleep**
you **didn't sleep**
he **didn't sleep**
she **didn't sleep**
it **didn't sleep**
we **didn't sleep**
you **didn't sleep**
they **didn't sleep**

See back cover.

5 Make the sentences negative.

▶ Splodge's rabbit ran upstairs.

Splodge's rabbit .didn't run....... upstairs.

1 It ate an apple.

It .... an apple.

2 Ruff went shopping.

Ruff .... shopping.

3 Tumble did the washing-up.

Tumble .... the washing-up.

4 Mildred drove the car.

Mildred .... the car.

D

Question	Short answer		
Did I **go?**	Yes, I **did.**	OR	No, I **didn't.**
Did you **go?**	Yes, you **did.**	OR	No, you **didn't.**
Did he **go?**	Yes, he **did.**	OR	No, he **didn't.**
Did she **go?**	Yes, she **did.**	OR	No, she **didn't.**
Did it **go?**	Yes, it **did.**	OR	No, it **didn't.**
Did we **go?**	Yes, we **did.**	OR	No, we **didn't.**
Did you **go?**	Yes, you **did.**	OR	No, you **didn't.**
Did they **go?**	Yes, they **did.**	OR	No, they **didn't.**

6 Read and answer the questions.

▶ Did you make a milkshake this morning?

Yes, I did... OR No, I didn't.

1 Did you have breakfast this morning?

....

2 Did your teacher go on holiday last week?

....

3 Did you meet a penguin yesterday?

....

4 Did you have an English lesson yesterday?

....

7

a Read the story. Circle all the verbs in the past simple.

Yesterday afternoon Lionel and Splodge (were) at the zoo. First, they went to see the elephants. The elephants had very big ears and they made strange noises with their long noses. Lionel said that elephants ran very fast. Splodge thought that was impossible. 'They're too big to run fast,' he said.

Then Lionel took Splodge to see the dolphins. The dolphins swam in their pool and did tricks. Splodge gave the dolphins some fish. They ate the fish very quickly. Splodge was hungry but he didn't think the fish were good to eat so they went to the shop at the zoo.

Lionel and Splodge bought two very big chocolate and strawberry ice creams. Then they stood and ate them next to the monkeys' cage.

How many verbs are there in the past simple?

....

b Now answer the questions.

► Where were Lionel and Splodge yesterday?

They were at the zoo.

1 Which animals did they see first?

....

2 Did the elephants have small ears?

....

3 What did Lionel say about the elephants?

....

4 Did Splodge believe Lionel?

....

5 Where did Lionel take Splodge next?

....

6 What did the dolphins do?

....

7 What did Splodge give the dolphins?

....

8 Splodge was hungry. Where did they go next?

....

9 What did Lionel and Splodge buy at the shop?

....

....

10 Where did Lionel and Splodge stand?

....

c Work with a partner. Take turns to ask and answer the questions in **7b**.

► Partner A   *Where were Lionel and Splodge yesterday?*
  Partner B   *They were at the zoo.*

  Partner B   *Which animals did they see first?*
  Partner A   *They …*

8 Fill in the gaps. Use the past simple of the words in brackets ( ).

Ruff Hello, Splodge. ▶ *Did* you *have* (have) a nice time?

Splodge Yes, I did. We (1) .... (go) to see a film. Then I (2) .... (be) hungry so we (3) .... (run) to the Mud Pie Café.

Ruff You're always hungry! (4) .... you .... (eat) a lot?

Splodge Yes, I did. I (5) .... (eat) a double mud pie and some chips. Then I (6) .... (drink) a big glass of Green Pea Milkshake. It (7) .... (be) delicious.

Ruff (8) .... you .... (go) shopping?

Splodge Yes, we did. Lionel (9) .... (drive) me in his car to the sweet shop and I (10) .... (buy) ten carrot lollipops for my rabbit.

Ruff (11) .... you .... (have) enough money?

Splodge No, I didn't. Lionel (12) .... (give) me some money. I like Lionel. (13) .... you .... (meet) him a long time ago?

Ruff No, because he didn't live in Wibble. He (14) .... (come) here from the South Pole last month.

Splodge That's a long way! (15) .... he .... (swim) across the sea?

Ruff No, of course not. I think he drove here in his new car, Splodge.

9

a Answer the questions.

▶ When did you get up?

I got up at seven o'clock.

Who made your breakfast this morning?

I made my breakfast this morning.

1 What did you eat for supper last night?

....

2 What did you drink?

....

3 What lessons did you have yesterday?

....

4 What was the last book you read?

....

5 Who was the first person you saw today?

....

6 When was your birthday?

....

7 Who gave you a present?

....

8 Did you go to a shop last week?

....

9 What did you buy?

....

10 When was the last time you went swimming?

....

b Work with a partner. Take turns to ask and answer the questions in **9a**.

▶ Partner A   *When did you get up?*
Partner B   *I got up at seven o'clock.*

Partner B   *Who made your breakfast this morning?*
Partner A   *My mother …*

Now write five questions to ask two other pupils.

▶ Did you go on holiday last year?

Did you read a book yesterday?

Did you go to the cinema last week?

....

....

....

....

....

▶ Pupil A   *Did you go on holiday last year?*
Pupil C   *Yes, I did. I went to the beach.*

Pupil B   *Did you read a book yesterday?*
Pupil D   *No, I didn't.*

10 Test yourself! Play in two teams. Your teacher says a verb. Say the past simple form. You get one point for every correct answer. You lose a point for every wrong answer.

▶ Teacher   *I read.*
Pupil   *I read.*   (Team scores one point.)

Teacher   *I sing.*
Pupil   *I sang.*   (Team scores one point.)

Teacher   *I think.*
Pupil   *I thinked.*   (Team loses a point!)

Going to 1

When I become the President tomorrow, I'm going to give everyone free chocolate and banana sandwiches!

Free chocolate and banana sandwiches? I'm going to vote for Tumble.

1 Tick (✔) the correct boxes.

• Is Tumble the President now?
Yes ☐   No ☐

• Does Tumble think he'll be the President tomorrow?
Yes ☐   No ☐

• Does Splodge want to vote for Tumble?
Yes ☐   No ☐

2 Write what Tumble is going to do.

► make the sun shine every day
He's going to make the sun shine every day.

1 open ice cream shops in every town
....
....

2 make lollipops grow on trees
....
....

3 organise trips to the moon
....
....

4 build chocolate houses
....
....

GRAMMAR

A

going to is for things you have decided to do in the future.

> *I'm going to give everyone chocolate and banana sandwiches.*
> *He's going to vote for Tumble.*
> *We're going to have a party tomorrow.*

B

Positive +

be + going to

I**'m going to**
you**'re going to**
he**'s going to**
she**'s going to**
it**'s going to**
we**'re going to**
you**'re going to**
they**'re going to**

3 Write what Tumble's friends are going to do.
Use **he's**, **she's** or **they're going to**.

▶ Ruff / help Tumble plant coconut trees

  He's going to help Tumble plant coconut trees.

1 Splodge / make sandwiches

  ....

2 Mabel / organise parties

  ....

3 Mildred / build a rocket

  ....

4 Ruff and Mabel / plant trees

  ....

C

Negative –

be + not going to

I**'m not going to**
you **aren't going to**
he **isn't going to**
she **isn't going to**
it **isn't going to**
we **aren't going to**
you **aren't going to**
they **aren't going to**

4 Look at the list below. Write four sentences to
say what you aren't going to do tomorrow.

travel to the moon ✔   cook a meal
go to the zoo   fly an aeroplane
go shopping   build a rocket
play football   do my homework
have lunch   go to New York
wash my hair   read a book

▶ *I'm not going to travel to the moon.* ....

  ....

  ....

  ....

  ....

D

Question	Short answer		
Am I **going to?**	Yes, I **am**.	OR	No, I**'m not**.
Are you **going to?**	Yes, you **are**.	OR	No, you **aren't**.
Is he **going to?**	Yes, he **is**.	OR	No, he **isn't**.
Is she **going to?**	Yes, she **is**.	OR	No, she **isn't**.
Is it **going to?**	Yes, it **is**.	OR	No, it **isn't**.
Are we **going to?**	Yes, we **are**.	OR	No, we **aren't**.
Are you **going to?**	Yes, you **are**.	OR	No, you **aren't**.
Are they **going to?**	Yes, they **are**.	OR	No, they **aren't**.

5 Fill in the gaps.

▶ *Is* ..... Ruff *going to* .... help

  Tumble with the party?

  (1) .... Splodge ....

  make some Fizzy Ink?

  (2) .... Mildred and Mabel

  .... buy the balloons?

  (3) .... Splodge ....

  cook some mud pies? (4) .... we

  .... play music at

  the party?

PRACTICE

6

a Look at Splodge's diary. What's he going to do?
Write your answers. Use **he's going to**.

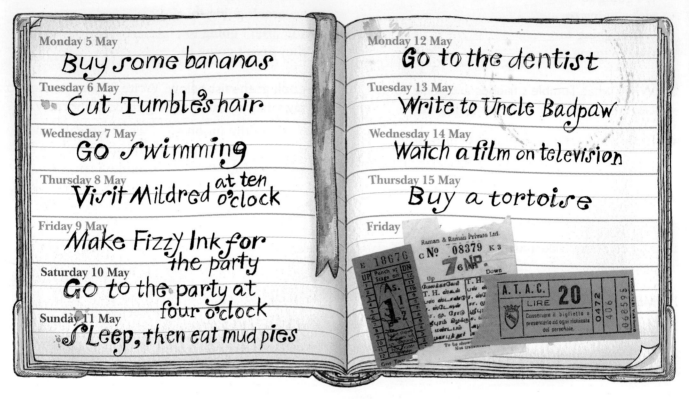

Monday 5 May
Buy some bananas

Tuesday 6 May
Cut Tumble's hair

Wednesday 7 May
Go swimming

Thursday 8 May
Visit Mildred at ten o'clock

Friday 9 May
Make Fizzy Ink for the party

Saturday 10 May
Go to the party at four o'clock

Sunday 11 May
Sleep, then eat mud pies

Monday 12 May
Go to the dentist

Tuesday 13 May
Write to Uncle Badpaw

Wednesday 14 May
Watch a film on television

Thursday 15 May
Buy a tortoise

Friday

▶ On Monday 5 May he's going to buy some bananas.

....

....

....

....

....

....

....

....

....

b Work with a partner. Take turns to ask and answer questions.

▶ Partner A   *What's Splodge going to do on the tenth of May?*
  Partner B   *He's going to go to the party.*

7 Match the sentences.

► Splodge has got a carrot.   They're going to have a bath.

1 I'm hungry.   He's going to drink some juice.

2 Mildred and Mabel are dirty.   She's going to pack a suitcase.

3 Ruff wants to buy a book.   He's going to feed his rabbit.

4 Tumble is thirsty.   I'm going to make a sandwich.

5 Mabel is going on holiday.   He's going to go to the bookshop.

---

6 Splodge's tooth hurts.   They're going to go to the doctor's.

7 Tumble is tired.   He's going to go swimming.

8 Mildred likes cooking.   He's going to go to bed.

9 Ruff and Splodge are ill.   He's going to go to the dentist's.

10 Splodge is going to the pool.   She's going to make a cake.

8

a Answer the questions. Use **going to**.

► What are you going to watch on television today?

I'm going to watch a cartoon.

1 What are you going to do tomorrow morning?

....

2 What are your friends going to do on Saturday?

....

3 What are you going to do this evening?

....

4 What lesson is your teacher going to teach next?

....

5 What are you going to eat for breakfast tomorrow?

....

6 Who are you going to speak to today?

....

b Work with a partner. Take turns to ask and answer
the questions in **8a**.

► Partner A   *What are you going to do tomorrow morning?*
  Partner B   *I'm going to go swimming with my brother.*

  Partner B   *What are you going to do tomorrow morning?*
  Partner A   *I'm going to go to the shops with my parents.*

9 Work with a partner. Pretend you're Tumble.
What are you going to do when you're the President?
Take turns to say sentences. Use some of the ideas below.

make the sun shine every day ✔
close the school on Thursdays ✔
have a party every Monday
give animals free rides on buses
plant coconut trees in every street
make green ice cream
give presents to every child
build lollipop castles
eat chocolate and banana sandwiches for lunch
build big playgrounds
give everyone free sweets

▶ Partner A   *I'm going to make the sun shine every day.*
Partner B   *I'm going to close the school on Thursdays.*

10

a Work in small groups. Choose one pupil in the group to be the President. Write ten things he or she is going to do.

▶ The President is going to close the school. ....

....

....

....

....

....

....

....

....

....

b Take turns to tell the class what you've written, like this:

▶ Pupil A   *The President is going to close the school.*
Pupil B   *The President is going to make homework easy.*
Pupil C   *The President is going to go to the moon.*

Going to 2

1   Tick (✔) the correct boxes.

• Will Mo fall? Yes ☐   No ☐

• How does Snapper know?
  Because he's clever. ☐
  Because he can see Spike cutting the tree down. ☐

GRAMMAR

A

going to is to talk about the future when you *know* what
will happen next. You know what will happen next because
of what you can see happening now.

> *Spike is cutting the tree. Mo is **going to** fall.*
> *The sun is shining. It's **going to** be a hot day.*

2   Fill in the gaps. Use **going to**.

▶   Mo is running towards the tree. He's ....going to.......... climb it.

1   Spike is cutting the tree down. It's .... fall.

2   Mo is falling. He's .... hurt himself.

3   There are big black clouds in the sky. It's .... rain.

4   I haven't done my homework. I'm .... get a bad mark.

B

Positive +

be + going to. It's easy!

I'm going to
he's/she's/it's going to
we're/you're/they're going to

C

Negative −

be + not going to

I'm not going to
he/she/it isn't going to
we/you/they aren't going to

D

Question	Short answer		
Am I **going to?**	Yes, I **am**.	OR	No, **I'm not**.
Is he/she/it **going to?**	Yes, he/she/it **is**.	OR	No, he/she/it **isn't**.
Are we/you/they **going to?**	Yes, we/you/they **are**.	OR	No, we/you/they **aren't**.

3 Match the sentences.

► Mo's sister is unhappy.   He's going to get fat.

1 It's raining.   She's going to cry.

2 Be careful! The ladder is broken.   He's going to have lunch.

3 He's making a sandwich.   We're going to get wet.

4 Snapper eats too much chocolate.   You're going to fall.

4 Complete Mo and Snapper's conversation. Use **be + not going to**.

Snapper   What shall we do? Pad is an hour late.

     ► He *isn't going to* .... come.

Mo   What shall we do? (1) We .... have any fun here. There's no one to play with.

Snapper   Let's go outside. It's sunny. (2) It .... rain.

Mo   But it's very windy, so it isn't going to be warm, and I haven't finished my homework.

Snapper   (3) Your teacher .... be happy.

Mo   I know. (4) I .... get a good mark.

Snapper   You never get a good mark, do you?

Mo   Be quiet, Snapper. Let's go outside and play.

5 Write the questions. Use the verbs below.

play   brush ✔   be   do   rain

► Snapper has got a toothbrush. *Is* .... he *going to brush* .... his teeth?

1 There are lots of clouds. .... it .... ?

2 It's half past eight. .... you .... late for school?

3 Mo has got a Maths book. .... he .... his homework?

4 They're wearing football boots. .... they .... football?

PRACTICE

6 Write sentences. Use **going to**.

▶ It's Monday morning.
Mo and Pad / go / to school.

Mo and Pad are going to go to school.

1 The bus is leaving.
They / miss / it.

....

2 Mo forgot to have breakfast.
He / be / hungry later.

....

3 The teacher is here.
The Maths lesson / start soon.

....

4 Mo hates Maths.
It / be / a difficult lesson.

....

5 The teacher has got a pen.
She / write / on the board.

....

6 Pad hasn't got his Maths book.
He / look at Mo's book.

....

7 Mo and Pad have got some sweets.
They / eat / them.

....

8 The teacher is testing the class.
She / ask / somebody a question.

....

9 Mo has got his hand in the air.
He / answer / the question.

....

10 It's nearly the end of the lesson.
The bell / ring.

....

7 Look at the pictures. What's going to happen next?

▶ They're going to fall off the bicycle.

1 ....

2 ....

3 ....

4 ....

5 ....

6 ....

7 ....

8 ....

9 ....

10 ....

8 Match the sentences.

▶ Mo and Snapper are running.

1 Snapper is playing with Mo's radio.

2 Mo's father is at the newsagent's.

3 Mo's sister is switching the television on.

4 Mo's mother is sitting in the sun.

5 Mo and his family are packing their suitcases.

She's going to get very hot.

They're going to go on holiday.

He's going to break it.

They're going to get tired.

She's going to watch a cartoon.

He's going to buy a newspaper.

6 Pad draws good pictures.

7 Mo doesn't do his homework.

8 Mo is wrapping a present.

9 Mo's mother is going to the post office.

10 Snapper and Mo are in the sweet shop.

He isn't going to pass his tests.

She's going to post a letter.

He's going to give it to Snapper.

They're going to buy some sweets.

He's going to win the prize for Art.

3 .... I ....
....
No, you aren't. You don't understand Maths.

4 .... she ....
....
Yes, she is. She's buying a cinema ticket.

5 .... it ....
....
No, it isn't. It's going to be hot and sunny.

6 .... he ....
....
No, he isn't. He doesn't like homework.

7 .... Spike ....
....
Yes, he is. I'm eating his sweets.

8 .... they ....
....
Yes, they are. They're at the bicycle shop now.

9 .... Snapper ....
....
No, he isn't. He can't find his towel.

10 .... she ....
....
Yes, she is. She's very thirsty.

9 Write the questions for these answers.
Use the words below.

buy Mo a bicycle   see a film   be late
make a cake ✔   drink some water
win the football match   be angry
rain tomorrow   pass my Maths test
go swimming   do his homework

▶ Are...... we going to make a cake? ....

Yes, we are. Here's some flour, some sugar

and two eggs.

1 .... those boys ....

.... No, they aren't.

They aren't playing very well.

2 .... we ....
Yes, we are. It's half past ten.

10 Work in two teams. Your teacher will say
these sentences. Say what you think is going to
happen next. Score one point for each correct
sentence.

There's no petrol in the car.
Mo's dog can see a cat.
It's midnight. Snapper and Mo aren't asleep.
Snapper is switching the television on.
I'm packing a suitcase.
Mo's mother is standing at the bus stop.
Snapper is chasing Mo.

▶ Teacher   *There's no petrol in the car.*
Team A   *It's going to stop.*
Team B   *It isn't going to work.*

REVISION 5 – be; there's and there are; have got

1 Write the positive (+) forms of **be** in the present simple.

I ....   we ....

you ....   you ....

he ....   they ....

she ....

it ....

2 Now write the negative (–) forms of **be** in the present simple.

I ....   we ....

you ....   you ....

he ....   they ....

she ....

it ....

3 Read the examples and cross out the wrong words below.

There's a machine in the kitchen.
There are test tubes in the lab.

Use **there's** with singular / plural nouns.

Use **there are** with singular / plural nouns.

4 What are the negative forms of **there's** and **there are**?

....

....

5 Read the sentence and answer the questions.

Splodge has got a rabbit but he hasn't got a cat.

What does Splodge own?

....

What doesn't Splodge own?

....

6 Read the examples and tick the correct box below.

Mildred has got a long nose.
I've got fair hair.
Sticky has got black ears.

You can use **have got** to describe people and animals.
True ☐   False ☐

7 Write the positive (+) forms of **have got**.

I ....   we ....

you ....   you ....

he ....   they ....

she ....

it ....

8 Write the negative (–) forms of **have got**.

I ....   we ....

you ....   you ....

he ....   they ....

she ....

it ....

9 Write the positive (+) forms of **be** in the past simple.

I/he/she/it ....

we/you/they ....

10 Write the negative (–) forms of **be** in the past simple.

I/he/she/it ....

we/you/they ....

REVISION 6 – present and past tenses

1 Read the story and tick the correct box.

Splodge's friend gets up at six o'clock every day. He always washes his hands and brushes his ears before he has breakfast. After breakfast he sings a funny song. Then he goes to school.

The present simple is to talk about things …
you're doing now. ☐
you do again and again. ☐

2 Write the positive (+) forms of the verb **eat** in the present simple.

I/we/you/they ....

he/she/it ....

3 Write the negative (–) forms of the verb **play** in the present simple.

I/we/you/they ....

he/she/it ....

4 Read the examples and tick two boxes.

He likes food and he likes cooking.
I love the sun and I love sunbathing.
We hate water and we hate swimming.

After **like**, **love** and **hate** you can use …
a noun. ☐
an adverb. ☐
an **ing** form. ☐

5 Read and answer the questions.

Splodge eats bananas for lunch.
Look! Ruff is eating a banana.

Is Splodge eating a banana now?
Yes ☐   No ☐

Is Ruff eating a banana now?
Yes ☐   No ☐

6 Write the positive (+) forms of the verb **work** in the present continuous.

I ....

we/you/they ....

he/she/it ....

7 Write the negative (–) forms of the verb **sing** in the present continuous.

I ....

we/you/they ....

he/she/it ....

8 Read the examples and tick the correct box.

Splodge helped Ruff yesterday.
We went on holiday last year.

The past simple is to talk about things …
that are happening now. ☐
that happened before now. ☐

9 Make the positive (+) forms of these verbs in the past simple.

help   ....

smile   ....

study   ....

stop   ....

go   ....

be   ....

10 Make the negative (–) forms of these verbs in the past simple.

help   ....

smile   ....

study   ....

stop   ....

go   ....

be   ....

27 Ability

1 Tick (✔) the correct box.

Can Mo read?   Yes ☐   No ☐

GRAMMAR

A

can is to say that you know how to do something.

> *I **can** swim.*
> *You **can** run fast.*
> *She **can** dance.*
> *We **can** read.*

2 Write four things you can do.
Use the words below to help you.

read ✔   swim   dance   count to ten
sleep   eat   drink   walk   run   play
write   speak English

▶ I can read. . . . .

. . . .

. . . .

. . . .

. . . .

B

can't is to say that you don't know how to do
something.

> *I **can't** fly.*   *You **can't** drive a car.*
> *He **can't** swim.*   *We **can't** run fast.*

3 Look at the list. What can't you do?
Write four sentences.

fly ✔   do Maths
speak fifteen languages   read a book
jump five metres   lift a bus
ride a bicycle   write backwards
talk   use a computer
run fast   play games
swim underwater   touch the ceiling

▶ I can't fly. . . . .

. . . .

. . . .

. . . .

. . . .

C

can is easy! It's the same for everybody.

Positive +	Negative –
I **can**	I **can't**
you **can**	you **can't**
he **can**	he **can't**
she **can**	she **can't**
it **can**	it **can't**
we **can**	we **can't**
you **can**	you **can't**
they **can**	they **can't**

4 Fill in the gaps.

▶ Can birds fly?   Yes, they *can* fly.

1 Can Mo read?   No, he .... read.

2 Can fish swim?   Yes, they .... swim.

3 Can you lift a bus?   No, I .... lift a bus.

4 Can you and your
friends write?   Yes, we .... write.

D

Question	Short answer
Can you read?	Yes, I **can**.
Can you fly?	No, I **can't**.
Can Snapper sing?	Yes, he **can**.
Can they dance?	No, they **can't**.

5 Write four questions to ask a friend what he or she can do.

▶ *Can you climb a tree?* ....

....

....

....

....

PRACTICE

6 Look at the animal quiz. Guess which sentences are true. Tick the correct boxes.

Now write sentences. Use **can** or **can't**.

▶ *A red kangaroo can jump twelve metres.* ....

1 ....

2 ....

3 ....

4 ....

5 ....

6 ....

7 ....

8 ....

9 ....

10 ....

TRUE FALSE

▶ A red kangaroo can jump twelve metres. ✔ ☐

1 Cats can climb trees. ☐ ☐

2 Rabbits can't hear. ☐ ☐

3 Killer whales can swim at 55 km an hour. ☐ ☐

4 Lions can read. ☐ ☐

5 Fleas can jump 33 cm. ☐ ☐

6 Mice can walk on two legs. ☐ ☐

7 Snails can sleep for three years. ☐ ☐

8 Cheetahs can run at 112 km an hour. ☐ ☐

9 Crocodiles can be six metres long. ☐ ☐

10 Elephants can't see. ☐ ☐

7

a Snapper is being silly.
He's asking Mo questions.
Write Mo's answers.
Use short answers.

▶ Can dogs sing?

No, they can't.

1 Can babies fly?

No, ...

2 Can you swim?

Yes, ...

3 Can I climb trees?

Yes, ...

4 Can children drive cars?

No, ...

5 Can we talk?

Yes, ...

6 Can your dad read?

Yes, ...

7 Can fish write?

No, ...

8 Can teachers read?

Yes, ...

9 Can your cat cook?

No, ...

10 Can girls play football?

Yes, ...

b Write five questions to ask a partner. Use **can**.

....

....

....

....

....

Now take turns to ask and answer your questions.

▶ Partner A   *Can Snapper talk?*
Partner B   *Yes, he can.*

Partner B   *Can you make a fire with two sticks?*
Partner A   *No, I can't.*

8

a Write five true sentences about things you can and can't do.
Then write five false sentences about things you can and can't do.

True

► I can play football.

I can't swim underwater.

....

....

....

....

False

I can walk on my hands.

I can't read.

....

....

....

....

b Work with a partner. Take turns to read your sentences to your
partner. Ask him or her to guess whether you are telling the truth
or not.

► Partner A   *I can walk on my hands.*
Partner B   *False.*

Partner A   *Yes, it's false.*
Partner B   *I can't swim underwater.*

9 Ask your teacher if you can play a class alphabet game.
Use **can** or **can't** and any person, animal or thing you
can think of. Play the game like this:

Pupil A   *Astronaut. An astronaut can walk on the moon.*
Pupil B   *Bear. A bear can't talk.*
Pupil C   *Crocodile. A crocodile can swim.*
Pupil D   *Dog. A dog can't read.*

10 Work with a partner or in small groups. Imagine you're
inventors. Invent two clever machines. Draw a picture of them on
a piece of paper. Write what each machine can do.

► A homework machine

It can do Maths and French.

It can get good marks.

It can help you.

A sweet machine

It can make a hundred sweets an hour.

It can make red and green sweets.

It can make chocolate.

Take turns to tell the class about your machines.

Permission

Hello, Tumble. I'm bored. **Can** I cook some mud pies? **Can** I have a mud bath?

No, Splodge, you **can't**. It's bedtime.

I Tick (✔) the correct boxes.

* Does Splodge want to cook mud pies?
Yes ☐   No ☐

* Does Tumble want Splodge to cook mud pies?
Yes ☐   No ☐

GRAMMAR

A

can is to ask someone a question when you want to do something and you want the answer to be 'Yes'.

Can I cook some mud pies?
Can my friend come to stay?
Can we go to the park?

2 Write Splodge's questions. Use **can I**.

▶ play with Ruff's machines
Can I play with Ruff's machines?

1 make a milkshake

....

2 cut Tumble's hair

....

3 go outside

....

4 watch television

....

B

Asking	Saying 'Yes'
Can I tell you a joke?	*Yes, you **can**.*
Can Ruff drive your car?	*Yes, he **can**.*
Can my friends come and see me?	*Yes, they **can**.*

3 It's Saturday. Splodge can do lots of things. He's asking questions. Write Tumble's answers. He says 'Yes'.

▶ Can I go out in Mabel's car?

    Yes, you can.

1 Can I play with my friends?

    ....

2 Can I go to the cinema?

    ....

3 Can I drink some Fizzy Ink?

    ....

4 Can my friends make mud pies?

    ....

C

Asking	Saying 'No'
Can I cut Tumble's hair?	*No, you **can't**.*
Can he play with your computer?	*No, he **can't**.*
Can my friends stay overnight?	*No, they **can't**.*

4 Read Splodge's questions. Write Tumble's answers. He says 'No'.

▶ Can I stay up till midnight?

    No, you can't.

1 Can I make a Green Pea Milkshake?

    ....

2 Can my friend drive Mabel's car?

    ....

3 Can I eat your cake?

    ....

4 Can I play music all night?

    ....

D

can is polite but if you want to be *very* polite use **could**.

> *Could I have some chocolate?*
> *Could we go to the cinema next week?*
> *Could my friend stay here tonight?*

5 Rewrite the sentences. Use **could**.

▶ Can I go outside?

    Could I go outside? ....

1 Can my friend come to lunch?

    ....

2 Can I play football this afternoon?

    ....

3 Can we make a cake?

    ....

4 Can I watch television?

    ....

6

a Splodge is asking Mabel and Mildred if he can do some things in their house. Mabel and Mildred always say 'No' to Splodge. Write ten questions.

put worms in your shoes ✔
build a rocket
play with your cat
climb the tree
use your telephone
drive your car
tell you a joke
make Fizzy Ink
eat your hat
glue your shoes to the floor
make a Green Pea Milkshake

▶ Can I put worms in your shoes? ....
....
....
....
....
....
....
....
....
....
....

b Work with a partner. Take turns to ask and answer the questions. Use **can I** and **yes, you can** or **no, you can't**.

▶ Partner A   *Can I put worms in your shoes?*
  Partner B   *No, you can't.*

7 Match the questions to the answers.

▶ Can I open my presents?

1 Can I make a sandwich?

2 Can I stay up till midnight?

3 Can I watch television?

4 Can I have a drink?

5 Can I drive the car?

No, you can't. You're too young to drive.

Yes, you can. There's milk in the fridge.

No, you can't. Go to bed.

No, you can't. There isn't any bread.

Yes, you can. It's your birthday.

Yes, you can. There's a cartoon on.

---

6 Can I buy a comic?

7 Can I stay at home tomorrow?

8 Can I telephone my friend?

9 Can I go outside?

10 Can I listen to some music?

No, you can't. You must go to school.

Yes, you can. Here's some money.

No, you can't. It's raining.

Yes, you can. The CD player is over there.

No, you can't. The telephone is broken.

8 Look at Splodge's secret code.

= G   = R = T

= Z = O = M

= I = S = W

= A = U = P

= F = D = L

= C = E = H

Here's Splodge's secret message.
Can you read it?

Write the message here:

□□□□ □□□
□□□□□ □
□□□□□ □□
□□ □□□ □□□
□□□□□□ ?

9

a You're asking your teacher these questions. Write what you think your teacher's answers are. Use **yes, you can** or **no, you can't**.

► Could we paint the classroom red?

Yes, you can. OR No, you can't.

1 Could we have longer breaks?

....

2 Could we have more English homework?

....

3 Could we draw on the board?

....

4 Could we use a dictionary?

....

5 Could we have less homework?

....

6 Could we have lessons at the weekend?

....

7 Could we play football in class?

....

8 Could we have shorter lessons?

....

9 Could we learn more grammar?

....

10 Could we help you tidy the classroom?

....

b Now take turns round the class to ask your teacher the questions. Listen carefully! Were your answers right?

10 Imagine you haven't done your Maths homework. Write a very polite note (maximum twenty words) to your Maths teacher. Ask if you can do the homework tomorrow.

Dear Teacher

....

....

....

....

11 Are you as polite as Splodge? Read his letter. Then work in small groups. Write ten things you would like to do at school on the lines below. Use **could we**.

> Could we have our lessons outside?
>
> ....
>
> ....
>
> ....
>
> ....

Could we make chocolate biscuits in class?

....

....

....

....

Requests

Speech bubbles in illustration:

*Tumble, **can** you pass me a fork?*
***Can** you put some cheese on my plate, please?*

*Ruff, **can** you ask the waiter for a spoon?*
***Could** you pass me a napkin, please?*

I Tick (✔) the correct boxes.

- What's Splodge eating?
  Potatoes ☐   Spaghetti ☐   Rice ☐

- Is Splodge asking for help?
  Yes ☐   No ☐

 GRAMMAR

A

can is to ask someone to do something for you.

> ***Can** you help me?*
> ***Can** you pass me a fork, please?*
> ***Can** you give me some water?*

2 Write questions. Use **can you**.

▶ Pass me the salt.   Can you pass me the salt, please?

1 Give me a drink.   ....

2 Open the door.   ....

3 Give me the menu.   ....

4 Cut my meat.   ....

B

can is polite but if you want to be *very* polite, use **could**.

> ***Could*** *you pass me a napkin?*
> ***Could*** *you help me with my homework?*
> ***Could*** *you open the window, please?*

3 Rewrite Splodge's questions. Use **could**.

▶ Can you give me some more potatoes, please?

Could you give me some more potatoes, please?

1 Can you pass me the peas, please?

....

2 Can you give me some money?

....

3 Can you open this box for me, please?

....

4 Can you ask the waiter for some ice cream?

....

....

P PRACTICE

3

4

a Splodge is eating more food in the restaurant!
Write his questions. Use **can** and the words
below.

cut my meat ✔	ask the waiter for a knife
give me some juice	pass me the beans
get me some bread	pass me the pepper
tell me a story	read the menu to me
open the bottle	choose my vegetables
ask for some water	

▶ Can you cut my meat, please?

....

....

....

....

....

....

....

....

....

....

....

b Work with a partner. Take turns to ask more
questions. Use the words below to give you
some ideas, or make your own questions.

take my plate away ✔	give me some salad
pass me a knife	ask for some fruit
give me a drink	pass me the potatoes
give me a small plate	

▶ Partner A   *Can you take my plate away?*
   Partner B   *Can you get me a milkshake?*

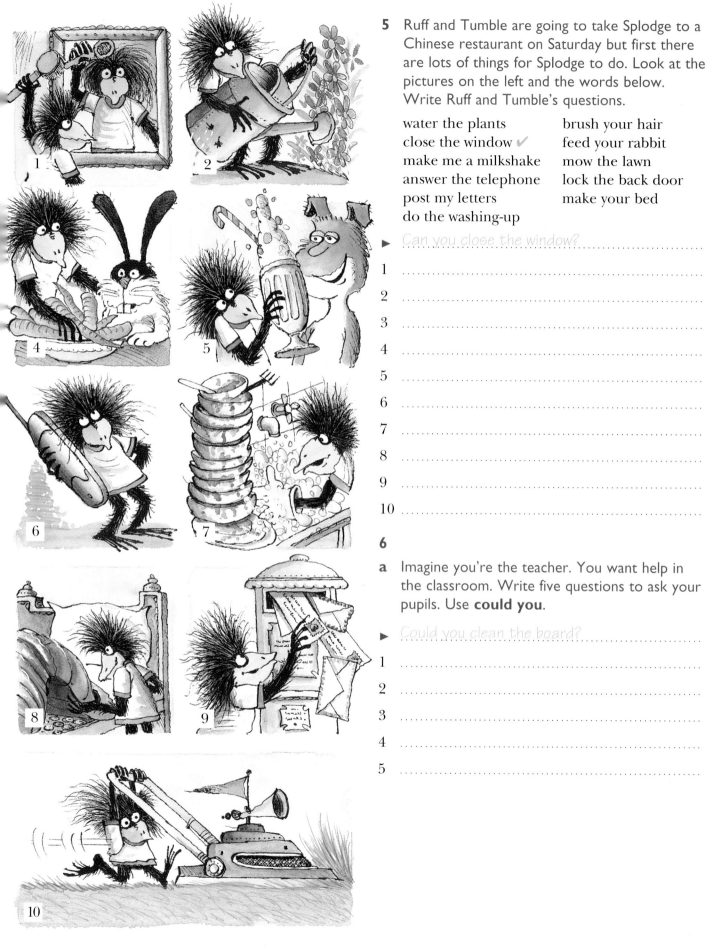

5 Ruff and Tumble are going to take Splodge to a Chinese restaurant on Saturday but first there are lots of things for Splodge to do. Look at the pictures on the left and the words below. Write Ruff and Tumble's questions.

water the plants   brush your hair
close the window ✔   feed your rabbit
make me a milkshake   mow the lawn
answer the telephone   lock the back door
post my letters   make your bed
do the washing-up

▶ *Can you close the window?* ....

1 ....

2 ....

3 ....

4 ....

5 ....

6 ....

7 ....

8 ....

9 ....

10 ....

6

a Imagine you're the teacher. You want help in the classroom. Write five questions to ask your pupils. Use **could you**.

▶ *Could you clean the board?* ....

1 ....

2 ....

3 ....

4 ....

5 ....

b Work with a partner. Take turns to ask each other to do five things and do them!

▶ Partner A   *Could you pass me a red pen, please?*
                  (Partner B, pass your friend a red pen.)
  Partner B   *Could you open my book, please?*
                  (Partner A, open your friend's book.)

7 Splodge and his friends are at the Chinese restaurant. Splodge has got a problem. He wants Tumble and Ruff to help him. Can you read the secret message?

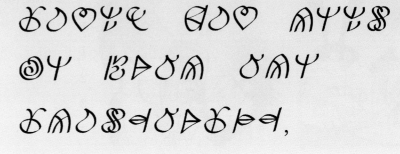

= A   = H

= M   = T

= C   = I

= O   = U

= D   = K

= P   = W

= E   = L

= S   = Y

Write the message here:

☐☐☐☐☐ ☐☐☐ ☐☐☐☐
☐☐ ☐☐☐☐ ☐☐☐
☐☐☐☐☐☐☐☐☐ ,
☐☐☐☐☐ ?

30 Obligation

Splodge, when you meet the King of Candaroon, you must bow three times with your eyes shut.

And you must wear red and blue socks.

1 Tick (✔) the correct boxes.

• Can Splodge bow with his eyes open when he meets the King?
Yes ☐   No ☐

• Can Splodge wear green socks?
Yes ☐   No ☐

GRAMMAR

A

must is to tell people what to do.

*You **must** bow three times.*
*You **must** wear red and blue socks.*
*You **must** shut your eyes.*

2 What does Ruff say to Splodge? Use **must**.

bow three times ✔   smile   be polite
answer the King's questions
say 'Hello, dear King'

►

1 ....

2 ....

3 ....

4 ....

B

must is easy!

you **must**
he **must**
she **must**
it **must**
you **must**
they **must**

3 Fill in the gaps. Use **must**.

The King of Candaroon says:

'Children ► ...must..... wear special clothes.

Boys (1) .... wear red and blue socks.

Girls (2) .... wear green and yellow

gloves. Children (3) .... be happy and

they (4) .... laugh at my jokes.'

 PRACTICE

4

a Read the Rules of Candaroon.

b Answer the questions.

► How many times must everybody bow to the King?

Everybody must bow three times.

1 What must cats do?

....

....

2 What must happen on Tuesdays?

....

....

3 Who must go swimming every day?

....

....

4 Who must be kind to Adverbs?

....

....

5 What must boys wear?

....

....

6 What language must everybody speak on Thursdays?

....

....

7 What must children eat for breakfast?

....

....

8 How many times must visitors knock at the castle door?

....

....

THE ELEVEN RULES OF
CANDAROON

Everybody must bow to the King three times.

Visitors must knock at the castle door five times.

Cats must wait outside the castle.

Boys must wear red and blue socks.

Children must eat peanuts for breakfast.

On Thursdays, everybody must speak Candarese.

Adults must always be kind to Adverbs.

Rabbits must have a bath every month.

Everybody, except the King, must walk backwards.

Girls must give the King a spider on Tuesdays.

Children must go swimming every day.

9 Who must walk backwards?

....

....

10 How often must rabbits have a bath?

....

....

c Work with a partner. Imagine you are the King of Candaroon. Write five more rules.

▶ *Everybody must wear green hats in winter.*

....

....

....

....

....

5

a Splodge wants to stay in Candaroon for a day. Imagine you're a guard. Tell him what to do. Make sentences. Use **must** and the words below.

▶ get up early   1 put your socks on
2 bring your rabbit   3 knock at the castle door   4 show your rabbit to the King
5 say the secret password
6 say your name   7 walk to the black door
8 open the green box   9 stand on your head
10 read the rules of Candaroon

▶ *You must get up early.*

1 ....

2 ....

3 ....

4 ....

5 ....

6 ....

7 ....

8 ....

9 ....

10 ....

b Work with a partner. Think about your parents and your teacher. What do they tell you to do? Take turns to say five sentences each.

▶ Partner A   *You must do your homework.*
Partner B   *You must go to bed at eight o'clock.*

Partner A   *You must listen in class.*
Partner B   *You must brush your teeth.*

6

a Work in small groups. Imagine a new country.

What's your country's name? ....

Has it got a King? ....

What's his name? ....

Now make rules for your country. Use **must**.

▶ *Everybody must wear yellow shoes.*
Children must eat chocolate for lunch.

1 ....

2 ....

3 ....

4 ....

5 ....

6 ....

7 ....

8 ....

9 ....

10 ....

b Now take turns to tell the class about your country's rules.

▶ Pupil A   *Our country is called Stickstock.*
Everybody must get up at night.
Adults must go to school.

Prohibition

1 Tick (✔) the correct boxes.

- Can Splodge drink the potion?
  Yes ☐   No ☐

- Can Splodge be noisy?
  Yes ☐   No ☐

GRAMMAR

A

mustn't is to tell somebody that they can't do something.

*You **mustn't** touch the test tubes.*
*You **mustn't** shout.*
*You **mustn't** drink Ruff's potions.*

2 Read what Ruff is saying. How many things mustn't Splodge do?

'Splodge, come here! You mustn't touch the test tubes. They're hot. Look at the bottles on the shelf. You mustn't open that small bottle. You mustn't drink the green potion because it makes you invisible. You mustn't shake the test tube and you mustn't play with the red powder. It's very dangerous.'

Splodge mustn't do .... things.

PRACTICE

3 Match the sentences.

▶ Don't use cold water.   You mustn't mix the ink and milk.

1 Don't stir the green powder.   You mustn't drop the blue bottle.

2 Don't talk to anyone.   You mustn't eat the magic beans.

3 Don't drop the blue bottle.   You mustn't talk to anyone.

4 Don't eat the magic beans.   You mustn't stir the green powder.

5 Don't mix the ink and milk.   You mustn't use cold water.

---

6 Don't drink the yellow water.   You mustn't say the magic spell.

7 Don't heat the test tube.   You mustn't give Splodge the recipe.

8 Don't say the magic spell.   You mustn't shake the bottle.

9 Don't shake the bottle.   You mustn't drink the yellow water.

10 Don't give Splodge the recipe. You mustn't heat the test tube.

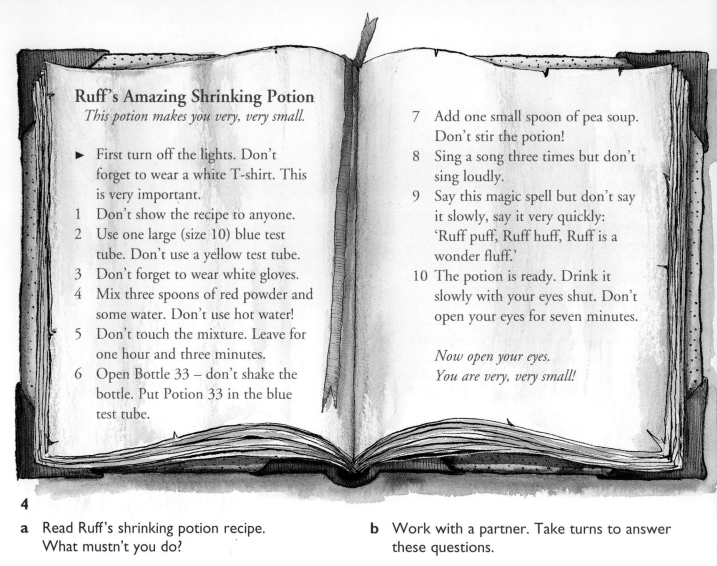

Ruff's Amazing Shrinking Potion
This potion makes you very, very small.

▶ First turn off the lights. Don't forget to wear a white T-shirt. This is very important.
1 Don't show the recipe to anyone.
2 Use one large (size 10) blue test tube. Don't use a yellow test tube.
3 Don't forget to wear white gloves.
4 Mix three spoons of red powder and some water. Don't use hot water!
5 Don't touch the mixture. Leave for one hour and three minutes.
6 Open Bottle 33 – don't shake the bottle. Put Potion 33 in the blue test tube.

7 Add one small spoon of pea soup. Don't stir the potion!
8 Sing a song three times but don't sing loudly.
9 Say this magic spell but don't say it slowly, say it very quickly: 'Ruff puff, Ruff huff, Ruff is a wonder fluff.'
10 The potion is ready. Drink it slowly with your eyes shut. Don't open your eyes for seven minutes.

Now open your eyes.
You are very, very small!

4

a Read Ruff's shrinking potion recipe. What mustn't you do?

▶ You mustn't forget to wear a white T-shirt.
1 ....
....
2 ....
3 ....
....
4 ....
5 ....
....
6 ....
7 ....
8 ....
9 ....
10 ....
....

b Work with a partner. Take turns to answer these questions.

What mustn't you forget to wear? ✔
What mustn't you show to anyone?
What test tube mustn't you use?
What colour gloves mustn't you forget to wear?
What water mustn't you use?
What mustn't you touch?
What mustn't you shake?
What mustn't you stir?
What mustn't you do loudly?
What mustn't you say slowly?
What mustn't you do for seven minutes?

▶ Partner A   *What mustn't you forget to wear?*
Partner B   *You mustn't forget to wear a white T-shirt.*

Partner B   *What mustn't you show to anyone?*
Partner A   *You mustn't show …*

5

a What do your teachers say you mustn't do at school? Make a list of ten things. Use the words below to help you.

eat in class   cheat   forget your books ✔
shout in class   draw pictures on the board
play football in your English lesson
sing in your Maths lesson   listen to music
stand on your desk   kick your friend
write on your desk

▶ You mustn't forget your books.

1 ....

....

2 ....

....

3 ....

....

4 ....

....

5 ....

....

6 ....

....

7 ....

....

8 ....

....

9 ....

....

10 ....

....

b Work with a partner. Imagine you are Ruff or Tumble. What do you think they say Splodge mustn't do in the house? Write ten sentences.

▶ You mustn't drink too much Fizzy Ink.
  You mustn't eat mud pies in the bath.

....

....

....

....

....

....

....

....

....

....

REVISION 7 – can, can't, could; must, mustn't

1 Read the sentence and tick the correct boxes.

Splodge can read but he can't swim.

Does Splodge know how to read?
Yes ☐   No ☐

Does Splodge know how to swim?
Yes ☐   No ☐

2 What can a bird do? Write two sentences.

....

....

3 What can't a fish do? Write two sentences.

....

....

4 Read what Splodge says and tick the correct box.

Can I watch television tonight?
Could I visit my friends tomorrow?

Who do you think Splodge is talking to?
Ruff ☐   A friend ☐

5 Tick the correct box. Think carefully.

can is more polite than **could**. ☐

could is more polite than **can**. ☐

6 Think of four things you want to do this weekend. Write four questions to ask your parents if you can do them. Use **can** and **could**.

....

....

....

....

7 Read the examples and tick the correct box.

Can you open the door, please?
Could you pass me a pen, please?

When you ask somebody to help you, you use …
can/could I. ☐
can/could you. ☐

8 Read the examples and cross out the wrong word in the rule.

Can you carry this box, please?
Could you carry this box, please?

Questions with **can** / **could** are more polite.

9 Read what Ruff says to Splodge and tick the correct boxes.

You must go to bed at nine.
You must do your homework now.

Can Splodge go to bed at ten?
Yes ☐   No ☐

Can Splodge do his homework tomorrow?
Yes ☐   No ☐

10 Read the examples and cross out the wrong word in the rule.

You mustn't shout in class.
You mustn't be rude.

mustn't is to tell somebody that

they can / can't do something.

11 What does your teacher say you must and mustn't do in class? Fill in the gaps. Use **must** or **mustn't**.

'You .... do your work.'

'You .... shout in class.'

'You .... be quiet.'

'You .... eat in class.'

Prepositions of place

> We must catch these prepositions, They're dangerous. Look! They're **on** the television, **in** the cupboard, **under** the table ...

1 Tick (✔) the correct box.

Where's Number 3?
On the table ☐ Under the carpet ☐
In the cupboard ☐

 **GRAMMAR**

A

Prepositions of place tell you *where* something is.

> *The book is **on** the table.*
> *Splodge is **in** the cupboard.*
> *We're **under** the stairs.*

2 Read the sentences carefully.
Circle the prepositions.

▶ Where's my watch? It's on the table.

1 Where's the toyshop? It's in Moon Street.

2 Where's Tumble's book? It's on the chair.

3 Where are Ruff's shoes? They're under the carpet.

4 Where's the milk? It's in the fridge.

B

These are prepositions of place:

on

in

behind

under

between

in front of

next to

3 Where are these prepositions? Look at the pictures above and write your answers.

► Number 1 is <u>behind</u> the fridge.

1 Number 7 is .... the cupboard.

2 Number 5 is .... the bed.

3 Number 9 is .... the table.

4 Number 6 is .... Splodge.

PRACTICE

4

a Look at the picture. Splodge is having tea with Mabel and Mildred. Fill in the gaps. Use prepositions.

Splodge is sitting ► <u>between</u> Mildred and Mabel. He's sitting (1) .... a chair. There's a tortoise (2) .... Mabel's chair and there's a cat sitting (3) .... the fire. There are three cups (4) .... the table. There's some tea (5) .... the cups. There are some chocolate biscuits (6) .... the teapot. Splodge has got a chocolate biscuit (7) .... his mouth. (8) .... Mabel there's a big plate of sandwiches. Mildred's parrot is standing (9) .... her head. He's got a piece of cake (10) .... his beak.

b Work with a partner. Take turns to ask and answer the questions.

▶ Where's Splodge?
1 Where's the tortoise?
2 Where's the cat?
3 How many cups are on the table?
4 Where are the chocolate biscuits?
5 Where's the parrot?

▶ Partner A *Where's Splodge?*
  Partner B *He's between Mabel and Mildred.*

5

a A friend of Splodge's lives in a town near Wibble. Look at the list of streets and places. Try to imagine the town. Where do you think everything is?

Streets	**Shops**	**Restaurants**	**Other places**
Moon Street	the post office	The Mud Pie Café	the park
Green Street	the bank	The Milkshake Bar	the school
Long Street	the toyshop		the station
Sunny Street	the sweet shop		
	the greengrocer's		
	the bakery		

b Now write ten sentences about the town. Use prepositions.

▶ The park is next to the school.
  The Mud Pie Café is next to the bank.
  The toyshop is in Moon Street.

....

....

....

....

....

....

....

....

6 Work with a partner. Take turns to put things in different places and ask your partner where they are. Use the suggestions below.

put your hands on your head ✔
put a book under your desk ✔
put your hands between your knees
stand next to your desk
put a pencil in your pencil case
hold a pen in your right hand
put your thumb in your mouth
put a book next to your chair
put a pencil between two books
stand next to the door

▶ Partner A *Where are my hands?*
  Partner B *They're on your head. Where's my book?*
  Partner A *It's under your desk.*

7

a Draw these things in the picture of Splodge's bedroom.

A teddy bear on Splodge's bed.
A cup between Splodge's toy box and the chair.
A football under Splodge's bed.
A cupboard next to Splodge's bed.
A radio in front of the cupboard.

A book on the table.
A bag behind the chair.
A cat in Splodge's toy box.
An apple under the chair.

b Listen to your teacher. Take turns to answer the questions.

► Teacher *Where's the teddy bear?*
  Pupil A *It's on Splodge's bed.*

8 Splodge is hiding. Can you read the secret code and find out where he is?

 = B   = H   = S ⌀ = D ᵟ = I

◇ = T ᵂ = E ᵇ = N ᵁ = U

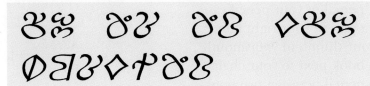

Write your answer here.

Prepositions of time

I Tick (✔) the correct boxes.

• Mo says his birthday is …
  in December. ☐   in August. ☐
  in June. ☐

• Do you think Mo is telling the truth?
  Yes ☐   No ☐

 GRAMMAR

A

Prepositions of time tell you *when* something happens.

These are prepositions of time: **in**, **on**, **at**

> *My birthday is **in** June.*
> *School starts **in** September.*
> *My birthday is **on** Wednesday.*
> ***On** Thursdays we play basketball.*
> *I was born **at** four o'clock.*
> *I have breakfast **at** seven o'clock.*

2 When's your birthday? Write the month.

My birthday is in ....

Now ask four friends when their birthday is.

Name	Month
...................'s birthday is in ....
...................'s birthday is in ....
...................'s birthday is in ....
...................'s birthday is in ....

B

in + month	in + year
in June, in September	*in 1965, in 2005*
*We have a holiday **in** June.*	*A man walked on the moon **in** 1969.*

3 Answer the questions. Use **in**.

How old will you be …

▶ in March?   In March............... I'll be ten years old.................

in September?   .... I'll be ....

in 2009?   .... I'll be ....

in February 2007? .... I'll be ....

in May next year? .... I'll be ....

C

on + day	on + date
on Monday	*on the fourth of September*
on Thursday	*on the tenth of October*

*Snapper will be ten years old **on** Friday.*
*There's a party **on** the ninth of January.*

4 Write sentences. Use **on**.

▶ There's a party / 9 January.

There's a party on 9 January........................

....

1 Mo goes back to school / 6 September.

....

....

2 Mo's mother is going to the supermarket / Monday.

....

....

3 Mo's father is playing tennis / Saturday morning.

....

....

4 Mo's mother starts a new job / 4 October.

....

....

D

at + clock time

*at four o'clock, **at** half past ten*

*I get up **at** half past seven.*
*She has lunch **at** one o'clock.*
*We go to bed **at** nine o'clock.*

5 Answer the questions. Use **at**.

▶ When do you have lunch?

I have lunch at half past twelve.................

1 When do you get up?

I get up ....

2 When does school start?

School starts ....

3 When do you have supper?

I have supper ....

4 When do you go to bed?

I go to bed ....

E

Be careful! Learn these:

in	**at**
in the morning	*at night*
in the afternoon	*at the weekend*
in the evening	*at lunchtime*

6 Fill in the gaps. Use **in** or **at**.

▶ In...... the morning Mo wakes up. He brushes his teeth (1) .... the morning and (2) .... night. He watches television (3) .... the weekend and (4) .... the afternoon when he comes home from school.

7

a Put the correct preposition of time under the headings.

+ month/year	+ day/date	+ time
....	....	....

b Tick (✔) the correct boxes.

▶ When's Milly's birthday?

At April ☐   In April ☑   On April ☐

1 When will Mo be twenty years old?

On 2010 ☐   In 2010 ☐   At 2010 ☐

2 When do you have breakfast?

On the morning ☐   At the morning ☐

In the morning ☐

3 When does the sun shine in England?

In July ☐   On July ☐   At July ☐

4 When do you play with your friends?

On the afternoon ☐   In the afternoon ☐

At the afternoon ☐

5 When do you have lunch?

In lunchtime ☐   At lunchtime ☐

On lunchtime ☐

c Work with a partner. Take turns to ask and answer the questions in **7b**.

▶ Partner A   *When's your birthday?*
  Partner B   *My birthday is in July.*

  Partner B   *When's your birthday?*
  Partner A   *My birthday is in November.*

8 When do you do the things below? Make two lists.

wake up ✔   have lunch ✔   go to sleep   go to school
see my friends   do a sport   do my homework   have breakfast
listen to music   watch television   get dressed   have a bath
read books   have supper   come home from school   go to the shops

in

▶ I wake up in the morning. ....

....

....

....

....

....

....

....

at

I have lunch at one o'clock. ....

....

....

....

....

....

....

....

9

a This is Mo's school timetable. Write what lessons he's got this week.
Use **on** and **at**. Write ten sentences.

	Monday	Tuesday	Wednesday	Thursday	Friday	Saturday
09.00	Maths	Biology	History	English	Art	Football
11.00	Art	Geography	French	French	Biology	
14.00	Chemistry	English	Maths	Music	History	

▶ On Monday at nine o'clock he's got a Maths lesson. ....

....

....

....

....

....

....

....

....

....

....

b Work with a partner. Look at your school timetables.
Take turns to say what lessons you've got every day.

▶ Partner A   *On Monday at ten o'clock we've got an English lesson.*
Partner B   *On Monday afternoon at three o'clock we've got
a Maths lesson.*

10 Read the sentences very carefully. Match the beginnings and ends.

▶ There's an Art lesson   on 9 January.

1 Mo's dad was born   1999.

2 It's Mo's birthday   six o'clock.

3 Mo's lesson   in 1969.

4 Snapper's party finishes at   on Monday.

5 Mo was nine years old in   starts at nine o'clock.

6 Mo is going on holiday   Tuesday.

7 It always rains in   at seven o'clock.

8 Mo isn't going to school on   match is on Saturday.

9 Snapper has supper   January.

10 The school football   in August.

11 Work in small groups or with a partner. Make as many sentences
as you can. Use the words below and **in**, **on** and **at**.

2011   lunchtime   Thursday   April   night
the afternoon   12 July   a quarter past three
the weekend   Sunday   midnight   November
the morning   the evening   Friday   January
five o'clock   22 May   September

▶ *On Thursday there's a basketball match.*
In April there are no lessons.
On Friday we're going to the moon.
We eat sandwiches at lunchtime.

Prepositions of movement

What's that thing? Look! It's coming out of the cupboard.

It's a preposition of movement. Look at that one. It's climbing up the curtain.

I like them. There's another one. It's jumping over the cat.

I Tick (✔) the correct boxes.

- What's Number 1 doing?
  Going into the cupboard ☐
  Coming out of the cupboard ☐

- What's Number 2 doing?
  Climbing up the curtain ☐
  Jumping over the cat ☐

GRAMMAR

A

Prepositions of movement tell you *how* things move and *where* they move to.

*It's coming **out of** the cupboard.*
*It's jumping **over** the cat.*
*It's climbing **up** the curtain.*
*It's running **from** the chair **to** the table.*

2 Circle the prepositions.

Splodge is frightened. There's a preposition running out of the cupboard. There's another one climbing up the curtain and there's one jumping over the cat. They move all the time. Splodge wants to jump over the prepositions, run out of the house and hide.

These are prepositions of movement:
into, **out of**; **up**, **down**; **over**, **round**; **from**, **to**

*Splodge is climbing **into** the cupboard.*

*Splodge is coming **out of** Sticky's box.*

*Splodge is going **up** the stairs.*

*Splodge is jumping **over** the wall.*

*Splodge is coming **down** the stairs.*

*Splodge is walking **round** the pond.*

*Splodge is walking **from** the tree **to** the bench.*

3 Answer the questions.
Tick the correct answers.

▶ Which things can you walk over?

a hill ☑   a bridge ☑   a city ☐

1 Which things can you go up?

a mountain ☐   a pond ☐   a ladder ☐

2 Which things can you go down?

a mouse ☐   a ladder ☐   the stairs ☐

3 Which things can you get into?

a box ☐   a wall ☐   a car ☐

4 Which things can you get out of?

a lift ☐   a car ☐   a table ☐

4 Splodge ran away from the prepositions. Look at the pictures and fill in the gaps.

▶ Splodge ran out of Mabel's house.

1 He went .... the garden.

2 He walked .... the flowerbed.

3 He fell .... the pond.

4 He jumped .... the pond at once.

5 He ran .... the pond .... the garden wall.

6 He climbed .... the ladder.

7 He climbed .... the wall.

8 He ran .... the street.

9 He went .... the sweet shop.

10 He ran .... the stairs and hid behind some lollipops.

5

a Splodge has drawn a treasure map. He's trying to explain it to Ruff and Tumble but he doesn't know any prepositions of movement. Fill in the gaps to help Ruff and Tumble understand the map.

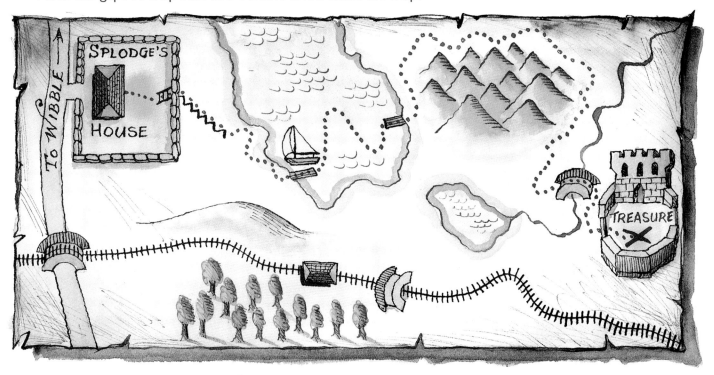

Start at our house. Go ▶ out of .... the back door. Now walk (1) ....

the back door (2) .... the garden wall. There's a ladder.

Climb (3) .... the ladder and go (4) .... the steps. Now walk

(5) .... the lake. There's a boat. Get (6) .... the boat and

sail (7) .... the mountains. Get (8) .... the boat and walk

(9) .... the mountains. You can see a castle and a bridge. Go

(10) .... the bridge to the castle. Dig a hole inside the castle.

The treasure is there!

b Work with a partner. Partner A, choose a place for the treasure but don't tell your partner. Now tell Partner B how to get to the treasure. When you've finished, swap.

▶ Partner A   *Start at Splodge's house. Go out of the front door and walk round the house. Walk over the hill and go to the station. The treasure is there.*

Partner B   *Start at the castle. Go out of the castle and over the bridge. Walk round the small lake and over the bridge. Go into the wood. The treasure is there.*

6 Ask your teacher if you can play this game. One pupil is Splodge. Take turns to tell Splodge what to do. Play the game like this:

Pupil A   *Splodge, walk from the board to the teacher.*
Pupil B   *Splodge, walk round a desk.*
Pupil C   *Splodge, go out of the classroom.*

When the pupil has done five things, he or she can choose another pupil to be Splodge.

REVISION 8 – prepositions

1 Read the examples and tick the correct box.

Splodge is sitting on a chair.
Tumble is hiding behind a tree.
Splodge's T-shirt is next to the bed.

Prepositions of place tell you …
when things are. ☐
where things are. ☐

2 Where's the ball? Fill in the gaps.

It's .... the box.

It's .... the box.

It's .... the box.

It's .... the box.

3 Read the examples and answer the question.

My birthday is on 15 July.
She was born in 1995.
I'm going to a party at four o'clock.

What three words can you use to say when things happen?

....

4 Read the examples and finish the rule.

My birthday is in June.
He invented the machine in 1999.

Use **in** with a .... and
a ....

5 Read the examples and tick two boxes.

He's going to a party on Monday.
His birthday is on 29 January.

Use **on** with …
years. ☐   days. ☐
months. ☐   dates. ☐

6 Read the examples and cross out the wrong words in the rule.

The match starts at ten o'clock.
I saw Ruff at three thirty.

Use **in / at / on** with a clock time.

7 Cross out the wrong words in the sentences.

I get up **at / in** the morning.

I sleep **at / in** night.

I see friends **in / at** the weekend.

8 Read the examples and tick the correct rule.

He ran from the house to the park.
The cat is climbing up the tree.
Splodge fell into the lake.

Prepositions of movement tell you …
when things happen. ☐
how things move and where they move to. ☐

9 Cross out the wrong words.

I ran **over / into** the kitchen.

He climbed **up / into** the stairs.

She went **down / round** the pond.

They jumped **over / under** the wall.

35 Questions 1

1 Tick (✔) the correct boxes.

• Does Splodge know where
  the zoo is?
  Yes ☐   No ☐

• Does Splodge know when
  the zoo opens?
  Yes ☐   No ☐

 GRAMMAR

A

Question words are to ask questions.

who is to ask about people. →	*Who are you?*
where is to ask about places. →	*Where's my hat?*
when is to ask about time. →	*When does the zoo open?*
why is to ask for a reason. →	*Why are you eating?*
how is to ask about the way to do something. →	*How do you make Fizzy Ink?*

2 Write the correct question word.

▶ *How*.......... do you make Fizzy Ink? Do you need lemonade?

1 .... is the zoo? Is it next to the station?

2 .... are you putting a coat on? Are you going out?

3 .... can we go? Can we go before lunch?

4 .... is upstairs? Is it Ruff?

B

Question	Verb	Subject	Verb
Who	*is*	*Mabel?*	
Where	*are*	*Tumble and Ruff?*	
When	*is*	*her birthday?*	
Who	*is*	*Mabel*	*watching?*
Where	*do*	*Mildred and Mabel*	*live?*
When	*do*	*you*	*wake up?*
Why	*are*	*they*	*laughing?*
How	*does*	*Splodge*	*sing?*

3 Fill in the gaps. Use the correct form of **be** or **do**.

Splodge Where ▶ .*do*........ kangaroos come from?

Ruff They come from Australia. Why (1) .... you buying

more sweets? You don't need them.

Splodge Shh! How (2) .... elephants drink?

Ruff They drink through their noses. Hurry up, Splodge. Why

(3) .... you eating so many sweets?

Splodge Because I'm a splodge. Splodges love sweets. Now, where

(4) .... the monkey house?

Ruff It's over there. But monkeys like sweets too so hide them!

C

how + adjective or adverb

	Adjective	
How	*tall*	*are you?*
How	*old*	*is Mildred?*
How	*clever*	*is Splodge?*

	Adverb	
How	*well*	*can you speak English?*
How	*fast*	*does Mabel's car go?*
How	*quickly*	*can you drink a glass of water?*

4 Choose the correct adjective or adverb from the words below.

slowly   old   tall   long ✔   fast

▶ How .*long*........ are a rabbit's ears?

They're about fifteen centimetres long.

1 How .... is that giant tortoise?

It's ninety years old.

2 How .... can a cheetah run?

One hundred and twelve kilometres an hour.

3 How .... does a snail move?

It moves about a metre in an hour.

4 How .... is a giraffe?

It's about five metres tall.

D

how many + nouns you can count

How many apples are there?
How many toys has Splodge got?
How many legs has a horse got?

how much + nouns you can't count

How much milk is there?
How much bread have we got?
How much cheese do we need?

See Chapter 7.

5 Write **how much** or **how many**.

► *How many* tigers are there at the zoo?

How much meat do they eat every day?

1 .... water does an elephant drink?

2 .... bananas do monkeys eat every day?

3 .... legs has a caterpillar got?

4 .... honey do bees make in a month?

PRACTICE

6 Splodge is talking to a meerkat at the zoo. Fill in his questions with the correct question word.

Splodge ► *Who* .... are you?

Meerkat I'm a meerkat. (1) .... are you?

Splodge I'm Splodge. (2) .... do you come from?

Meerkat I come from Africa.

Splodge (3) .... did you come to this zoo?

Meerkat Five years ago.

Splodge (4) .... do you stand on two legs?

Meerkat Because it's comfortable. I run on four legs.

Splodge (5) .... do you live?

Meerkat I live in that hole. It's nice and warm.

(6) .... do you live?

Splodge I live in a town called Wibble. (7) .... many

friends have you got at the zoo?

Meerkat Oh, lots. The tigers, the bears, the elephants, the

kangaroos, the penguins …

Splodge (8) .... is your best friend?

Meerkat A penguin called Lionel. Do you want to meet him?

Splodge Yes, please. (9) .... does he come from and

(10) .... do you like him?

Meerkat He comes from the South Pole. He's my best friend

because he's funny.

7 Fill in the gaps. Use the correct form of **be** or **do**.

Wibble Zoo

Questions for visitors

1 Where _____ camels come from?

2 When _____ the lions have supper?

3 Why _____ monkeys eat nuts?

4 Where _____ the tigers' cage?

5 Why _____ elephants so big?

6 When _____ the zoo-keeper start work?

7 How _____ fish breathe?

8 Where _____ the crocodiles?

9 When _____ the dolphin show starting?

10 Why _____ lions sleep all day?

8 Work with a partner. What questions would you like to ask Splodge? Write as many questions as possible. Use **who, where, when, why** and **how**.

▶ Why are you noisy?

Where do you come from?

Who's your best friend?

....

....

....

....

....

....

....

....

....

9 Read Tumble's answers. Now write Splodge's questions.

▶ Tigers come from India.

Where do tigers come from? ....

1 The zoo opens at nine o'clock.

When ....

2 Ruff is in the kitchen.

Where ....

3 I'm laughing because you're funny, Splodge.

Why ....

4 We're going at half past eight.

When ....

5 The shop is near the entrance to the zoo.

Where ....

6 It opens at eleven o'clock.

When ....

7 Hippos live in Africa.

Where ....

8 You can't touch the lions because they bite!

Why ....

9 The snakes are near the crocodile house.

Where ....

10 The penguins eat at six o'clock.

When ....

10

a Splodge wants to know more about the animal hiding in the cage.
He's talking to Alfred, the zoo-keeper. Write his questions.
Use **how** and the words in brackets.

Splodge ▶ How long are its ears? (long / ears)

Alfred Its ears are ten centimetres long.

Splodge How well can it hear? (well / hear)

Alfred It can hear very well. It's listening now.

Splodge (1) .... (fast / eat)

Alfred It eats very fast. It's always hungry.

Splodge (2) .... (fat)

Alfred It isn't fat, it's thin.

Splodge (3) .... (old)

Alfred It's three years old. It was born at the zoo.

Splodge (4) .... (fast / run)

Alfred It can run very fast, faster than you!

Splodge (5) .... (quickly / move)

Alfred It moves very quickly.

Splodge (6) .... (big / head)

Alfred Its head is quite small.

Splodge (7) .... (clever)

Alfred It's very clever.

Splodge (8) .... (dangerous)

Alfred It isn't very dangerous.
It doesn't bite.

Splodge (9) .... (long / tail)

Alfred Its tail is a metre long.

Splodge (10) .... (well / swim)

Alfred It can swim very well. It swims in this pool.

b Work with a partner. Think of an animal.
Don't tell your partner what your animal is!
Take turns to guess what the animal is.
Ask questions. Use **how**.

▶ Partner A *How tall is it?*
Partner B *It's about one metre tall.*
Partner A *How many legs has it got?*
Partner B *It's got two legs.*
Partner A *Is it a penguin?*
Partner B *Yes, it is.*

What's this?

It's an Eggbomb machine.

Whose machine is it?

It's Ruff's, of course!

36 ◆ Questions 2

1 Tick (✔) the correct boxes.

- Does Splodge know what the Eggbomb machine is?
  Yes ☐   No ☐

- Does he know who owns the machine?   Yes ☐   No ☐

GRAMMAR

A

Question words are to ask questions.

what is to find out more about people or things when there are many possible answers.

   What's your name? (There are lots of names.)

which is to ask the difference between two or more people or things when there aren't many possible answers.

   Which book is yours? (There are three books on the desk.)

whose is to ask who owns something.

   Whose machine is this? It's Ruff's machine.

2 Write **what**, **which** or **whose**.

▶ *What* .... is Splodge doing?

1 .... is this football?
  Is it yours?

2 .... colour is your jacket?

3 .... comic is Splodge's?
  This one or the comic on the table?

4 .... do you like eating?

B

what, **which**, **whose** + verb

> *What's your friend's name?*
> *Which is Splodge's T-shirt?*
> *Whose are these sweets?*

3 Put the words in the correct places.

▶ Ruff and Splodge   doing?   What   are

   What are Ruff and Splodge doing? . . . .

1 is   his   Which   bicycle?

   . . . .

2 these   toys?   Whose   are

   . . . .

3 name?   her   is   What

   . . . .

4 Which   your   house?   is

   . . . .

PRACTICE

5 Splodge is asking lots of questions. Fill in the gaps with **what**, **which** or **whose**.

▶ What . . . . is that machine?

   It's an Eggbomb machine.

1 . . . . does it make?

   It makes eggbombs, silly!

2 . . . . machine is it?

   It's Ruff's machine.

3 . . . . button do you press to make it start?

   The blue button.

4 . . . . sweets are those?

   They're Mabel's sweets.

5 . . . . part do the eggbombs come out of?

   The small hole at the front.

C

what, **which**, **whose** + noun + verb

	Noun	Verb	
What	*car*	*is*	*this?*
Which	*drink*	*is*	*mine?*
Whose	*potion*	*is*	*this?*

4 Look at the words below. Put them in the correct places.

   games   cat   city ✔   T-shirt   animal

▶ Which city . . . . is this? Rome or Cairo?

1 Which . . . . do you want?

   The green one or the red one?

2 What . . . . do you play?

3 Which . . . . is this? A crocodile
   or a giraffe?

4 Whose . . . . is this? Is it Mabel's?

6

a Fill in the gaps. Use **what**, **which** or **whose**.

Tumble ▶ _What_ ...... are you doing, Splodge?

Splodge I'm helping Ruff to make a machine.

Tumble (1) .... machine is he making today?

Splodge A Boomerang Biscuit machine. (2) .... colour shall I paint it? Blue, green or red?

Tumble Green. (3) .... does it do?

Splodge That's a silly question. It makes Boomerang Biscuits, of course!

Tumble (4) .... a boomerang?

Splodge It's a thing you throw and then it comes back to you.

Tumble (5) .... idea is this?

Splodge It's Ruff's idea. Now, (6) .... do I need?

Tumble Flour? Sugar? Nails? A hammer? (7) .... flavour are the biscuits?

Splodge I don't know. (8) .... do you like best? Chocolate or banana?

Tumble Banana. And (9) .... 's the name of the biscuits?

Splodge Banana Boomerang Biscuits.

Tumble That's a very good name. Splodge, (10) .... are these sweets? Are they yours?

Splodge Yes. They're my special brain sweets. They help me think about machines. Now, stop asking questions. I'm very busy!

b Work with a partner. Take turns to ask and answer the questions.

▶ What's Splodge doing?
1 Which colour is he going to paint the machine?
2 What does the machine make?
3 What's a boomerang?
4 Whose idea is the machine?
5 Which flavour does Tumble like? Chocolate or banana?
6 What's the name of the biscuits?
7 Whose are the sweets?
8 What sweets are they?

▶ Partner A   _What's Splodge doing?_
  Partner B   _He's helping Ruff to make a machine._

  Partner B   _Which colour is he going to paint the machine?_

  Partner A   _He's going to paint the machine ..._

b Work with a partner. Take turns to ask and answer the questions.

▶ Partner A   *What animal do you like?*
  Partner B   *I like tigers.*

  Partner B   *Which do you like: Maths or watching television?*
  Partner A   *I like Maths.*

8

a Write ten questions to ask a friend. Use **what** and **which**.

▶ *What's the time?*
....

Which day do you like most?
....

....

....

....

....

....

....

....

....

....

....

b Work with a partner. Take turns to ask and answer your questions.

▶ Partner A   *What's the time?*
  Partner B   *It's half past ten.*

  Partner B   *Which day do you like most?*
  Partner A   *I like Saturday most.*

9 Ask your teacher if you can play a class game. You must answer a question and then ask a new question. Play the game like this:

Teacher   *What's your favourite colour?*
Pupil A   *Green. What's the time?*
Pupil B   *Twelve o'clock. What colour is Ruff?*
Pupil C   *He's green. What day is it today?*
Pupil D   *It's Friday. What …*

7

a Read the questions. Write your answers on a piece of paper.

▶ What animal do you like?
  Which do you like: Maths or watching television?
1 Which colour do you like: red or blue?
2 Which is the biggest: a mouse, a dog or a horse?
3 What colour is the sky?
4 What's your favourite fruit?
5 Which do you like most: milk, water or orange juice?
6 What do you eat for breakfast?
7 Which does Splodge like: mud pies or lettuce?
8 What colour are your eyes?
9 Which is better: a schoolday or a holiday?
10 What's your favourite subject at school?

Short answers

1 Tick (✔) the correct boxes.

- Look at the first three pictures.
  Do you think Snapper is asleep?
  Yes, I do. ☐   No, I don't. ☐

- Are Mo and Snapper best friends?
  Yes, they are. ☐   No, they aren't. ☐

- Can Mo have Snapper's sweets?
  Yes, he can. ☐   No, he can't. ☐

GRAMMAR

REMEMBER!

These are subject pronouns.

   I, you, he, she, it, we, you, they

See Chapter 9.

2 Write four sentences using these subject pronouns.

▶ You're my friend.

1 He ....

2 I ....

3 We ....

4 They ....

A

Short answers are easier and quicker than long answers.
Look at these sentences.

Question	Long answer	Short answer
Are you asleep?	Yes, I'm asleep.	*Yes, I am.*
Can she hear me?	No, she can't hear you.	*No, she can't.*
Do you like Mo?	Yes, we like Mo.	*Yes, we do.*
Have they got any sweets?	No, they haven't got any sweets.	*No, they haven't.*

3 Read the conversation. Underline the short answers.

Snapper I'm ready to go. Are you ready?

Mo No, I'm not.

Snapper Are we going outside to play?

Mo No, we aren't.

Snapper Can we watch television?

Mo No, we can't.

Snapper Do you like me?

Mo Yes, I do.

Snapper Have you got any chocolate?

Mo No, I haven't!

B

Make short answers with a subject pronoun + **be**, **can**, **do** or **have**.
Pronoun + **be**

Question	Short answer
Are you asleep?	*Yes, I am.* OR *No, I'm not.*
Is Mo your friend?	*Yes, he is.* OR *No, he isn't.*

See also boxes C, D and E on page 162 for **can**, **do** and **have**.

4 Match the questions and short answers.

▶ Is Snapper asleep?   No, I'm not.

1 Is Mo a boy?   Yes, they are.

2 Is Mo's sister with him?   No, he isn't.

3 Are they in their house?   Yes, he is.

4 Are you asleep?   No, she isn't.

C

Pronoun + can

Question	Short answer
Can I have your sweets?	*Yes, you can.* OR *No, you can't.*
Can Snapper come to play?	*Yes, he can.* OR *No, he can't.*

5 Tick the correct boxes. Write short answers.

▶ Can Snapper play football?

Yes ☑   No ☐ Yes, he can.

1 Can dogs read?

Yes ☐   No ☐ ....

2 Can Mo have Snapper's sweets?

Yes ☐   No ☐ ....

3 Can you swim?

Yes ☐   No ☐ ....

4 Can you talk in class?

Yes ☐   No ☐ ....

D

Pronoun + do

Question	Short answer
Do you want Mo to be happy?	*Yes, I do.* OR *No, I don't.*
Does he play football?	*Yes, he does.* OR *No, he doesn't.*

6 Write short answers to the questions.

▶ Do you like cartoons?

Yes, I do. OR No I don't. ....

1 Do you like lettuce?

....

2 Do your friends like playing games?

....

3 Does your teacher read comics?

....

4 Do your parents drink coffee?

....

E

Pronoun + have

Question	Short answer
Have you got a best friend?	*Yes, I have.* OR *No, I haven't.*
Has Snapper got some sweets?	*Yes, he has.* OR *No, he hasn't.*

7 Answer the questions.

▶ Have you got a pet? Yes, I have. ....

1 Have your parents got a car?

....

2 Has your friend got a bicycle?

....

3 Have you got five legs?

....

4 Has your doctor got brown hair?

....

PRACTICE

8

a Fill in the gaps with short answers. Use a pronoun + **be** or **can**.

Mo   Snapper, are you watching television?

Snapper   No, ▶ *I'm not.*

Mo   Are you going to play outside?

Snapper   Yes, ...

Mo   Can I come with you?

Snapper   No, ... I don't like you.

Mo   Are you angry with me?

Snapper   Yes, ... You've got my sweets.

Mo   Can I give you a present?

Snapper   Yes, ...

Mo   Are you angry with me now?

Snapper   No, ...

b Work with a partner. Take turns to ask and answer the questions.

1   Are you at school now?
2   Can you swim?
3   Is your name Snapper?
4   Can your parents use a computer?
5   Are you ten years old?
6   Can you play tennis?
7   Is English your favourite subject?
8   Can I copy your homework?
9   Are cats nicer than dogs?
10 Can I have your lunch?

▶   Partner A   *Are you at school now?*
     Partner B   *Yes, I am. Can you swim?*
     Partner A   *Yes, I can.*

9

a Look at Snapper's quiz. Tick the correct boxes.

		Yes	No
▶	Do dogs read books?	☐	☑
1	Do elephants drink water?	☐	☐
2	Can you read English?	☐	☐
3	Have spiders got six legs?	☐	☐
4	Is a mouse bigger than a fly?	☐	☐
5	Is a fly smaller than an ant?	☐	☐
6	Has your friend got green hands?	☐	☐
7	Does your best friend like milk?	☐	☐
8	Can cats talk?	☐	☐
9	Are you happy?	☐	☐
10	Do rabbits eat meat?	☐	☐

b Now write the short answers.

▶   *No, they don't.* ....

1   ....

2   ....

3   ....

4   ....

5   ....

6   ....

7   ....

8   ....

9   ....

10 ....

10

a In the left-hand column, write ten questions to ask a partner.
Ask about his or her age, height, clothes, toys, home, family, pets
etc. Use **be**, **can**, **do** and **have**. Don't write the answers yet.

Questions   **Answers**

▶ Are you ten years old?   Yes, I am.

  Can your parents speak English?   Yes, they can.

  Do you like bananas?   Yes, I do.

  Have you got brothers or sisters?   No, I haven't.

1 ....

2 ....

3 ....

4 ....

5 ....

6 ....

7 ....

8 ....

9 ....

10 ....

b Now work with a partner. Ask your questions and write his or
her answers in the right-hand column.

11 Ask your teacher if you can play a guessing game.
One pupil thinks of an animal, for example an elephant. The class
tries to guess what the animal is. This is how you play:

▶ Pupil A   *I'm big.*
  Class   *Are you a horse?*
  Pupil A   *No, I'm not. I'm grey.*
  Class   *Are you an elephant?*
  Pupil A   *Yes, I am.*

Reference

Here are some things you need to remember.

A

What are **vowels**? They're these letters:

a, e, i, o, u

B

What are **consonants**? They're these letters:

b, c, d, f, g, h, j, k, l, m, n, p, q, r, s, t, v, w, x, y, z

C

What are **nouns**? They're names for people, animals, things and places.

Splodge is funny.   *This is a **book**.*
*I like **penguins**.*   *We live in **London**.*

D

What are **articles**? **A** and **an** are articles. They go with nouns.

*Lionel is **a** penguin.*
*I can see **an** elephant.*

E

What are **pronouns**? They're words that replace nouns.

Ruff invents things.   → ***He** invents things.*
Splodge likes **biscuits**.   → *Splodge likes **them**.*
Mabel likes **animals**.   → ***She** likes **them**.*
This is **my book**.   → *This is **mine**.*

F

What are **adjectives**? They're words that tell you more about nouns.

It's a cat.   → *It's a **big** cat.*
This is a flower.   → *This is a **beautiful** flower.*
Splodge likes dogs. → *He likes **small** dogs.*

G

What are **verbs**? They're words to talk about things you do.

*Ruff **is making** a new machine.*
*Splodge **eats** mud pies.*
*Lionel the penguin **lives** in Wibble Zoo.*
*Penguins **can swim**.*
*Tumble **is washing** his hands.*
*Mabel **talks** to her parrot.*

H

What are **adverbs of manner**? They're words that tell you more about verbs.

Splodge eats.   → *Splodge eats **quickly**.*
Lionel swims.   → *Lionel swims **well**.*

What are **adverbs of frequency**? They're words that tell you when something happens.

We read books.   → *We **often** read books.*
Ruff is busy.   → *Ruff is **always** busy.*

I

What are **prepositions**?
They're words that do three things.

They tell you:

1   where things are.
*Splodge is **on** the bed.*
*Ruff is **in** the kitchen.*

2   how things move and where they move to.
*Splodge is running **down** the stairs.*
*He walks **into** the park and **over** the bridge.*

3   when things happen.
*It's Tumble's birthday **on** Tuesday.*
*We go to school **at** eight o'clock.*
***In** summer I go swimming.*

J

How do all these words work? They make **sentences**. Look at these sentences.

Noun	Verb	Article	Noun
Sticky	*is*	*a*	*rabbit.*

Noun	Verb	Article	Adjective	Noun
Sticky	*is*	*a*	*nice*	*rabbit.*

Pronoun	Verb	Article	Adjective	Noun
He	*is*	*a*	*nice*	*rabbit.*

Noun	Verb	Preposition	Article	Noun
Sticky	*is*	*in*	*the*	*cupboard.*

Noun	Verb	Adverb
Sticky	*runs*	*fast.*

K

What are **capitals** and **full stops**?

1   Sentences start with a **capital** letter and end with a **full stop**.

Capital letters are BIG letters.

This is a full stop: **.**

The rabbit is sitting on Splodge's bed.

2   Names of people and places start with a **capital** letter.

We love Splodge.
Splodge lives in a town called Wibble.
They're going to Spain.
London is in England.

L

Nouns are often the **subject** or **object** of a sentence.
Read the sentences. Then answer the questions.

Subject noun

Splodge	*plays a lot.*	Who plays?	....
Ruff	*reads every day.*	Who reads?	....
Rabbits	*eat at night.*	What eats?	....

Subject noun   **Object noun**

Splodge	*plays*	*games.*	What does he play?	....
Ruff	*reads*	*books.*	What does he read?	....
Rabbits	*eat*	*carrots.*	What do they eat?	....

REVISION 9 – questions

1 Look at the sentences and answer the questions.

'*Who's that?*' '*It's Splodge.*'
'*Where's Ruff?*' '*He's in the lab.*'
'*When are we going?*' '*At four.*'

Which word is to ask about time?

....

Which word is to ask about places?

....

Which word is to ask about people?

....

2 Read the examples and finish the rule.

Who's in the garden?
Who does this rabbit belong to?
Why is Splodge laughing?
Where does Mabel live?
How is Tumble today?
When does the shop open?

The verbs .... and ....

come after **who**, **where**, **when**, **why** and **how**.

3 Read the examples and finish the rule.

How tall are you?
How quickly can you run?

You can put an adjective or an

.... after **how**.

4 Read the examples and tick the correct boxes.

How many sweets does he eat?
How much water does he drink?

Use **how many** with …
nouns you can count.   ☐
nouns you can't count.   ☐

Use **how much** with …
nouns you can count.   ☐
nouns you can't count.   ☐

5 Read the examples and cross out the wrong words in the rule.

Which car do you like – the red one or the blue one?
Which do you want – a cheese sandwich, a biscuit or an apple?

Use **which** when there are

lots of / two or three possible answers.

6 Fill in the gaps. Use **what** or **which**.

.... is the time?

.... book is yours – this one or that one?

.... cat do you like – the black one or

the brown one?

.... is your favourite colour?

7 Read the examples and tick the correct box.

Whose is this comic? It's Splodge's.
Whose potion is this? It's Ruff's.

Whose is to ask …
where something is.   ☐
who owns something.   ☐

8 Fill in the gaps. Use the correct question word.

.... old are you?

.... is Ruff? I can't see him.

.... are you doing?

.... much honey is there?

.... does the train leave?

At nine o'clock.

.... many toys has he got?

.... can't cats fly?

Because they haven't got wings.

Useful words

Aa

actor [noun] ....

add [verb] ....

adult [noun] ....

angry [adjective] ....

ant [noun] ....

art [noun] ....

artist [noun] ....

Bb

backwards [adverb] ....

balloon [noun] ....

bark [verb] ....

beak [noun] ....

bean [noun] ....

behave [verb] ....

believe [verb] ....

boomerang [noun] ....

bored [adjective] ....

boring [adjective] ....

bow [verb] ....

brain [noun] ....

breathe [verb] ....

bridge [noun] ....

builder [noun] ....

Cc

cabbage [noun] ....

cage [noun] ....

cartoon [noun] ....

castle [noun] ....

catch [verb] ....

caterpillar [noun] ....

cheetah [noun] ....

chef [noun] ....

climb [verb] ....

cloud [noun] ....

coin [noun] ....

Dd (comfortable section)

comfortable [adjective] ....

comic [noun] ....

complete [verb] ....

conduct [verb] ....

correct [adjective] ....

correct [verb] ....

count [verb] ....

country [noun] ....

Dd

dangerous [adjective] ....

delicious [adjective] ....

describe [verb] ....

diary [noun] ....

dirty [adjective] ....

double [verb] ....

drive [verb] ....

drop [verb] ....

Ee

easily [adverb] ....

easy [adjective] ....

enormous [adjective] ....

exactly [adverb] ....

Ff

factory [noun] ....

famous [adjective] ....

favourite [adjective] ....

feed [verb] ....

fizzy [adjective] ....

flavour [noun] ....

flea [noun] ....

flour [noun] ....

fly [verb] ....

forget [verb] ....

free [adjective] ....

funfair [noun] ....

fur [noun] ....

Gg

gallery [noun] ....

glove [noun] ....

glue [noun] ....

guess [verb] ....

Hh

hammer [noun] ....

handsome [adjective] ....

heavy [adjective] ....

hill [noun] ....

hole [noun] ....

horrible [adjective] ....

hungry [adjective] ....

hunt [verb] ....

hurt [verb] ....

Ii

imagine [verb] ....

impossible [adjective] ....

ink [noun] ....

instrument [noun] ....

interesting [adjective] ....

invent [verb] ....

inventor [noun] ....

invisible [adjective] ....

invite [verb] ....

island [noun] ....

Jj

judge [noun] ....

Kk

kind [adjective] ....

knock [verb] ....

Ll

ladder [noun] ....

lake [noun] ....

lawn [noun] ....

leave [verb] ....

lettuce [noun] ....

life [noun] ....

lift [verb] ....

loaf [noun] ....

lollipop [noun] ....

loudly [adverb] ....

Mm

machine [noun] ....

marble [noun] ....

medicine [noun] ....

meet [verb] ....

menu [noun] ....

messy [adjective] ....

midnight [noun] ....

mix [verb] ....

mixture [noun] ....

mow [verb] ....

mud [noun] ....

Nn

nail [noun] ....

napkin [noun] ....

nasty [adjective] ....

naughty [adjective] ....

necklace [noun] ....

neighbour [noun] ....

noisy [adjective] ....

nurse [noun] ....

Oo

octopus [noun] ....

orchestra [noun] ....

organize [verb] ....

outside [adverb] ....

owl [noun] ....

own [verb] ....

Pp

peanut [noun] ....

petrol [noun] ....

pineapple [noun] ....

planet [noun] ....

plate [noun] ....

playground [noun] ....

poet [noun] ....

polite [adjective] ....

pool [noun] ....

pot [noun] ....

potion [noun] ....

powder [noun] ....

prize [noun] ....

puzzle [noun] ....

Rr

recipe [noun] ....

replace [verb] ....

rice [noun] ....

rule [noun] ....

Ss

sailor [noun] ....

salt [noun] ....

scientist [noun] ....

scream [verb] ....

secret [adjective] ....

secretary [noun] ....

shake [verb] ....

shower [noun] ....

shrink [verb] ....

slide [noun] ....

smash [verb] ....

snail [noun] ....

soldier [noun] ....

spell [noun] ....

spoon [noun] ....

statue [noun] ....

stay [verb] ....

stick [noun] ....

stick [verb] ....

stir [verb] ....

strange [adjective] ....

subject [noun] ....

suitcase [noun] ....

swap [verb] ....

swing [noun] ....

switch on/off [verb] ....

Tt

tail [noun] ....

taste [verb] ....

terrible [adjective] ....

test tube [noun] ....

theatre [noun] ....

thirsty [adjective] ....

throw [verb] ....

thumb [noun] ....

timetable [noun] ....

tired [adjective] ....

toast [noun] ....

together [adverb] ....

touch [verb] ....

towel [noun] ....

trousers [noun] ....

Uu

ugly [adjective] ....

umbrella [noun] ....

uncle [noun] ....

uniform [noun] ....

untidy [adjective] ....

use [verb] ....

Vv

vegetable [noun] ....

vet [noun] ....

visitor [noun] ....

vote [verb] ....

Ww

waiter [noun] ....

warm [adjective] ....

windy [adjective] ....

worm [noun] ....

Present forms of verbs

Long forms		Short forms		Questions
Present simple of be (see Chapter 14)				
I am	I am not	I'm	I'm not	Am I?
you are	you are not	you're	you aren't	Are you?
he is	he is not	he's	he isn't	Is he?
she is	she is not	she's	she isn't	Is she?
it is	it is not	it's	it isn't	Is it?
we are	we are not	we're	we aren't	Are we?
you are	you are not	you're	you aren't	Are you?
they are	they are not	they're	they aren't	Are they?
Present simple of have got (see Chapter 16)				
I have got	I have not got	I've got	I haven't got	Have I got?
you have got	you have not got	you've got	you haven't got	Have you got?
he has got	he has not got	he's got	he hasn't got	Has he got?
she has got	she has not got	she's got	she hasn't got	Has she got?
it has got	it has not got	it's got	it hasn't got	Has it got?
we have got	we have not got	we've got	we haven't got	Have we got?
you have got	you have not got	you've got	you haven't got	Have you got?
they have got	they have not got	they've got	they haven't got	Have they got?

Long forms		Short forms		Questions
Present simple (see Chapters 18, 19 and 21)				
I like	I do not like		I don't like	Do I like?
you like	you do not like		you don't like	Do you like?
he likes	he does not like		he doesn't like	Does he like?
she likes	she does not like		she doesn't like	Does she like?
it likes	it does not like		it doesn't like	Does it like?
we like	we do not like		we don't like	Do we like?
you like	you do not like		you don't like	Do you like?
they like	they do not like		they don't like	Do they like?
Present continuous (see Chapters 20 and 21)				
I am working	I am not working	I'm working	I'm not working	Am I working?
you are working	you are not working	you're working	you aren't working	Are you working?
he is working	he is not working	he's working	he isn't working	Is he working?
she is working	she is not working	she's working	she isn't working	Is she working?
it is working	it is not working	it's working	it isn't working	Is it working?
we are working	we are not working	we're working	we aren't working	Are we working?
you are working	you are not working	you're working	you aren't working	Are you working?
they are working	they are not working	they're working	they aren't working	Are they working?